PENGUIN BOOKS

THE PENGUIN BOOK OF NONSENSE VERSE

Quentin Blake was born in 1932 in the suburbs of London. He read English at Downing College, Cambridge, and Education at London University; at the same time he was beginning his career as a cartoonist and illustrator for *Punch*, the *Spectator* and other magazines. With his work for children's books, which include both his own stories as well as collaborations with Roald Dahl, Russell Hoban, Joan Aiken, Michael Rosen, John Yeoman and other writers, he has become one of the best-known contemporary illustrators. He has also illustrated books for adults such as, most recently, Cyrano de Bergerac's *Voyages to the Sun and Moon* for the Folio Society.

In 1965 Quentin Blake joined the staff of the Royal College of Art, where he was head of the Illustration Department from 1978 to 1986, and where he is now Visiting Professor. He was made an O B E in 1988.

THE
PENGUIN
BOOK OF
NONSENSE VERSE

SELECTED AND ILLUSTRATED BY

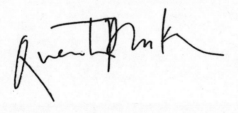

PENGUIN BOOKS

PENGUIN BOOKS

Published by the Penguin Group

Penguin Books Ltd, 27 Wrights Lane, London W8 5TZ, England

Penguin Books USA Inc., 375 Hudson Street, New York, New York 10014, USA

Penguin Books Australia Ltd, Ringwood, Victoria, Australia

Penguin Books Canada Ltd, 10 Alcorn Avenue, Toronto, Ontario, Canada M4V 3B2

Penguin Books (NZ) Ltd, 182–190 Wairau Road, Auckland 10, New Zealand

Penguin Books Ltd, Registered Offices: Harmondsworth, Middlesex, England

First published as *The Quentin Blake Book of Nonsense Verse* by Viking 1994

Published under the present title in Penguin Books 1995

3 5 7 9 10 8 6 4 2

The acknowledgements on pp. 285–6 constitute an extension of this copyright page

The moral right of the author has been asserted

Printed in England by Clays Ltd, St Ives plce

Contents

————

INTRODUCTION

Would I make my own choice of poems for a book of nonsense verse? And then would I illustrate it? An invitation as attractive as that doesn't happen very often, so I said 'yes' straight away. After that I had to think what I knew about nonsense.

I've certainly had some dealings with it at one time and another; and there does seem to be some natural affinity between nonsense in words and nonsense in pictures. It's something I first noticed many years ago when I was still a schoolboy. I had gone to stay with some family friends in the country. They had three small children, and I found myself making drawings to amuse them. Here's a giant to begin with – not too difficult. But should he have one head or two? I seem to remember that in the end we decided that three looked best. And then this dragon: five legs? seventeen? why not twenty-two? With socks on, of course. What we were happily launched into was the experimental non-sense of suppose-we-make-it-different.

This is nothing new. Hundreds of years ago people were writing nonsense based on a version of just this idea; of standing things on their heads; of the world-turned-upside-down. The result may be exactly the opposite of what we're used to – so that there's a pig cooking a man, instead of the other way about – or it may be something quite incongruous, like a goat playing the violin. This is very nice if you are an illustrator, because you are given a lot of new and amusing subjects to draw. The same is not true about another way of standing things on their heads, which is to write about things which can't be drawn because, except in words, they can't *be*. You can find it today in the playground:

> *I went to the pictures tomorrow*
> *And took a front seat at the back*

but it, too, is not a new invention.

There is another aspect of the nonsensical suppose-we-make-it-different experiment that didn't show itself until later on, in the nineteenth century. It was the idea of making up new words; words like *frabjous* and *vorpal*, which sound as though they mean something but actually don't. Did the urge to do this come into being because printing was becoming more common, words were being organized into dictionaries, and so at least a few writers began to feel that a little anarchy was called for?

(These words I've quoted, incidentally, are from 'Jabberwocky'. In it Lewis Carroll invented, and obviously enjoyed inventing, a whole string of new words. The strange thing is that some of them, like *chortle*, *galumphing* and *burble*, have passed into the language, so that plenty of people now use them without knowing where they come from or that they were ever meant to be nonsense in the first place.)

The first two sections of this book are devoted to these two kinds of nonsense – the world-turned-upside-down kind and the invented-words kind – but all the other sections are simply based on the idea of putting similar things together, such as animals, birds, travels, successes, confusions, and so on, in a way that I thought would be interesting. I can't guarantee that every poem I've included is pure nonsense. Some have an element of nonsense without being absolutely nonsensical; and there are a few that are just sort of crazy in a way that I couldn't resist, like the poem about 'Snaix'. Worse than that, I've also cheated and put in one or two poems that are not nonsense at all, but just *look* like nonsense. 'I saw a Peacock' stops being nonsense if you move the punctuation to the middle of the line. The poem 'Belagcholly Days' looks as though it's composed of a lot of those invented words until you say it as if you had a cold in your nose. (The last word is *Aðieu*, but you have to sneeze at the same time.) And there *may* be others.

There is one respect in which nonsense poetry isn't in the least bit crazy; the rhymes, the metre, the verse-forms are just as regular as, and in many cases identical with, those of more serious poems. Indeed, it's the fact that nonsense poems preserve this decorum – that at first sight they appear to be serious – that makes them effective. More than that it allows them, sometimes, to have their own mysterious poetry and atmosphere, so that they are funny and serious at the same time.

When I began collecting the poems for this book I was already in possession of a piece of encouraging good fortune. I had a rich source of verses in the books of several people whose work I had illustrated, such as Margaret Mahy, Russell Hoban, Ogden Nash and Roald Dahl; so that the beginning was easy. But after having started at home, so to speak, the subsequent search went into all kinds of places; not only into libraries and bookshops but also among the stray dis-pirited volumes loitering on the shelves of spare bedrooms: anywhere that nonsense might lurk. I looked at all kinds of anthologies and at the works of individual poets; everything from leather-bound to paperback. One very helpful book turned up unexpectedly just at the right moment, in a second-hand bookshop in New Orleans, where it seemed to have been waiting for me. And, to end as well as to begin with luck, on three occasions when I thought there *ought* to be poems which, however, didn't exist, John Yeoman, with characteristic promptness, sat down and wrote them for me.

Looking back at the collection of books I've searched through I'm reminded once again of the affinity between nonsense writing and nonsense drawing, because a number of the authors quoted here were or are also distinguished artists. Edward Lear is the most famous example, but there are also Mervyn Peake and Edward Gorey, and several others. However, for this collection, because we wanted it to be a book in its own right and come together as a single entertainment, you will find that you have my illustrations all the way through. I hope you will like them too.

The World Turned Upside Down

from

THE WORLD TURNED UPSIDE DOWN

OR,

NO NEWS, AND STRANGE NEWS

———

Here you may see what's very rare,
  The world turn'd upside down;
A tree and castle in the air,
  A man walk on his crown.

To see a cat catching a mouse,
        is no news;
But to see a rat building a house,
        is strange indeed!

Some rats take delight to gnaw
  Houses down –
I want to build a good
  House of my own.

To see a bird picking at fruit,
   is no news;
But to see a dog playing the flute,
   is strange indeed!

You see I am playing here,
 Too, too, too, too;
When I've done with my flute,
 I'll give it to you.

To see a man get a boat,
   is no news;
But to see a man jump down his throat,
   is strange indeed!

If I once get my legs in
 As far as my knees,
The rest will slip down
 With a great deal of ease.

To see a good boy read his book,
   is no news;
But to see a goose roasting a cook,
   is strange indeed!

I'll roast ye, and baste ye,
But who will may taste ye.

To see a boy swim in a brook,
          is no news;
But to see a fish catch a man with a hook,
          is strange indeed!

Spare me, good Mr Fish,
   I didn't molest you.
I'll spare you no longer
   Than till I dress you.

To hear a parrot say, pretty Poll,
          is no news;
But to see a sow with a parasol,
          is strange indeed!

Like a lady I shine,
   I'm so fat and so fine;
I've a right I suppose,
   To a shade for my nose.

ANONYMOUS

I SAW A PEACOCK

I saw a peacock with a fiery tail
I saw a blazing comet pour down hail
I saw a cloud all wrapt with ivy round
I saw a lofty oak creep on the ground
I saw a beetle swallow up a whale
I saw a foaming sea brimful of ale
I saw a pewter cup sixteen feet deep
I saw a well full of men's tears that weep
I saw wet eyes in flames of living fire
I saw a house as high as the moon and higher
I saw the glorious sun at deep midnight
I saw the man who saw this wondrous sight.

ANONYMOUS

Uptown, Downtown

Uptown, downtown,
Wrong side to,
Goodness me
What a hullabaloo!

Upstairs, downstairs,
Roundabout,
Backwards, forwards,
Inside OUT!

CLYDE WATSON

ONE FINE DAY IN THE MIDDLE
OF THE NIGHT

———————

One fine day in the middle of the night,
Two dead men got up to fight,
Back to back they faced each other,
Drew their swords and shot each other.
A paralysed donkey passing by
Kicked a blind man in the eye,
Knocked him through a nine-inch wall
Into a dry ditch and drowned them all.

ANONYMOUS

I SAW IIJ HEDLES PLAYEN AT A BALL

———————

I saw iij hedles playen at a ball,
an hanlas man served hem all,
Whyll iij movthles men lay & low,
iij legles a-way hem drow.

ANONYMOUS

26

I went to the pictures tomorrow
I took a front seat at the back,
I fell from the pit to the gallery
And broke a front bone in my back.
A lady she gave me some chocolate,
I ate it and gave it her back.
I phoned for a taxi and walked it,
And that's why I never came back.

PLAYGROUND RHYME

TOPSYTURVEY-WORLD

If the butterfly courted the bee,
    And the owl the porcupine;
If churches were built in the sea,
    And three times one was nine;
If the pony rode his master,
    If the buttercups ate the cows,
If the cat had the dire disaster
    To be worried, sir, by the mouse;
If mamma, sir, sold the baby
    To a gipsy for half a crown;

If a gentleman, sir, was a lady,
   The world would be Upside-Down!
If any or all of these wonders
   Should ever come about,
I should not consider them blunders,
   For I should be Inside-Out!

WILLIAM BRIGHTY RANDS

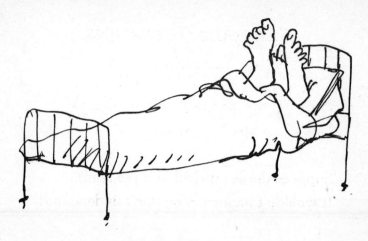

WHEN I WENT OUT FOR A WALK
ONE DAY

When I went out for a walk one day,
   My head fell off and rolled away,
And when I saw that it was gone –
   I picked it up and put it on.

When I went into the street
   Someone shouted, 'Look at your feet!'
I looked at them and sadly said,
   'I've left them both asleep in bed!'

ANONYMOUS

SENSIBLE QUESTIONS

'Suppose the land turned into the sea?'
'Don't be stupid! It couldn't be!'

'Suppose the sea turned into the land?'
'It wouldn't happen. You don't understand!'

'Suppose I waved this grassy stalk,
And Max the dog began to talk?'

'Your fancy's foolish. Your ways are wild!
I often think you're a silly child!'

But Marigold waved her stalk of grass
And all she had asked about came to pass.

The land rolled up and the sea rolled over
The waves were covered with grass and clover,

While Marigold and her reproving aunt
Who'd kept on saying 'Don't!' and 'Can't!',

Were up to their necks in a wild green sea –
And Max the dog said, 'Fiddle dee dee!'

MARGARET MAHY

CHORTLING AND GALUMPHING

JABBERWOCKY

'Twas brillig, and the slithy toves
   Did gyre and gimble in the wabe;
All mimsy were the borogoves,
    And the mome raths outgrabe.

'Beware the Jabberwock, my son!
   The jaws that bite, the claws that catch!
Beware the Jubjub bird, and shun
    The frumious Bandersnatch!'

He took his vorpal sword in hand:
   Long time the manxome foe he sought –
So rested he by the Tumtum tree,
    And stood awhile in thought.

And as in uffish thought he stood,
   The Jabberwock, with eyes of flame,
Came whiffling through the tulgey wood,
    And burbled as it came!

One, two! One, two! And through and through
   The vorpal blade went snicker-snack!
He left it dead, and with its head
   He went galumphing back.

'And hast thou slain the Jabberwock?
   Come to my arms, my beamish boy!
O frabjous day! Callooh! Callay!'
   He chortled in his joy.

'Twas brillig, and the slithy toves
   Did gyre and gimble in the wabe;
All mimsy were the borogoves,
   And the mome raths outgrabe.

LEWIS CARROLL

36

TO MARIE

When the breeze from the bluebottle's blustering
  blim
    Twirls the toads in a tooroomaloo,
And the whiskery whine of the wheedlesome whim
    Drowns the roll of the rattatattoo,
Then I dream in the shade of the shally-go-shee,
    And the voice of the bally-molay
Brings the smell of the pale poppy-cod's blummered
  blee
    From the willy-wad over the way.

Ah, the shuddering shoe and the blinketty-blanks
    When the punglung falls from the bough
In the blast of a hurricane's hicketty-hanks
    O'er the hills of the hocketty-how!
Give the rigamarole to the clangery-whang,
    If they care for such fiddlededee;
But the thingumbob kiss of the whangery-bang
    Keeps the higgledy-piggle for me.

L'Envoi

It is pilly-po-doddle and aligobung
    When the lollypup covers the ground,
Yet the poldiddle perishes plunkety-pung
    When the heart jimny-coggles around.
If the soul cannot snoop at the gigglesome cart
    Seeking surcease in gluggety-glug,
It is useless to say to the pulsating heart,
    'Yankee-doodle ker-chuggety-chug!'

ANONYMOUS

TYPO

'Nitgub,' said the typewriter,
and clenched the paper tight.
'Nitgub positively.
It is here in black and white.'
'Nonsense,' I said.
'I typed N-O-T-H-I-N-G;
the word of course was *nothing*,
simply nothing, don't you see?'
'Nothing may be what you meant,
but *nitgub's* what you wrote.
I like it,' said the typewriter.
'It strikes a happy note.
It has more style than *nothing*,
has a different sort of sound.
The colour is superior;
the flavour's nice and round.
Have you plumbed its deepest depths,
its mystery explained?'
'All right,' I·said, 'I'll take it.
Nitgub ventured, nitgub gained.'

RUSSELL HOBAN

THE LUGUBRIOUS WHING-WHANG

Out on the margin of moonshine land,
   Tickle me, love, in these lonesome ribs,
Out where the whing-whang loves to stand,
Writing his name with his tail on the sand,
And wiping it out with his oogerish hand;
   Tickle me, love, in these lonesome ribs.

Is it the gibber of gungs and keeks?
   Tickle me, love, in these lonesome ribs,
Or what *is* the sound the whing-whang seeks,
Crouching low by the winding creeks,
And holding his breath for weeks and weeks?
   Tickle me, love, in these lonesome ribs.

Aroint him the wraithest of wraithly things!

    Tickle me, love, in these lonesome ribs,

'T is a fair whing-whangess with phosphor rings,

And bridal jewels of fangs and stings,

And she sits and as sadly and softly sings

As the mildewed whir of her own dead wings;

    Tickle me, dear; tickle me here;

    Tickle me, love, in these lonesome ribs.

JAMES WHITCOMB RILEY

BELAGCHOLLY DAYS

Chilly Dovebber with his boadigg blast
  Dow cubs add strips the bedow add the lawd,
Eved October's suddy days are past –
      Add Subber's gawd!

I kdow dot what it is to which I cligg
  That stirs to sogg add sorrow, yet I trust
That still I sigg, but as the liddets sigg –
      Because I bust.

Add now, farewell to roses add to birds,
  To larded fields and tigkligg streablets eke;
Farewell to all articulated words
      I fain would speak.

Farewell, by cherished strolliggs od the sward,
  Greed glades and forest shades, farewell to you;
With sorrowing heart I, wretched add forlord,
      Bid you – achew!!!

ANONYMOUS

A RECIPE FOR INDIGESTION

DILLY DILLY PICCALILLI

Dilly Dilly Piccalilli
Tell me something very silly:
There was a chap his name was Bert
He ate the buttons off his shirt.

CLYDE WATSON

EVER EATEN

Ever eaten
poodle strudel?

It's sensational
with cream

I once had
chihuahua cheesecake

(Or was that
another bad dream?)

ROGER MCGOUGH

BLEEZER'S ICE-CREAM

I am Ebenezer Bleezer,
I run BLEEZER'S ICE-CREAM STORE,
there are flavours in my freezer
you have never seen before,
twenty-eight divine creations
too delicious to resist,
why not do yourself a favour,
try the flavours on my list:

COCOA MOCHA MACARONI
TAPIOCA SMOKED BALONEY
CHECKERBERRY CHEDDAR CHEW
CHICKEN CHERRY HONEYDEW
TUTTI-FRUTTI STEWED TOMATO
TUNA TACO BAKED POTATO
LOBSTER LITCHI LIMA BEAN
MOZZARELLA MANGOSTEEN
ALMOND HAM MERINGUE SALAMI
YAM ANCHOVY PRUNE PASTRAMI
SASSAFRAS SOUVLAKI HASH
SUKIYAKI SUCCOTASH

BUTTER BRICKLE PEPPER PICKLE
POMEGRANATE PUMPERNICKEL
PEACH PIMENTO PIZZA PLUM
PEANUT PUMPKIN BUBBLEGUM
BROCCOLI BANANA BLUSTER
CHOCOLATE CHOP SUEY CLUSTER
AVOCADO BRUSSELS SPROUT
PERIWINKLE SAUERKRAUT
COTTON CANDY CARROT CUSTARD
CAULIFLOWER COLA MUSTARD
ONION DUMPLING DOUBLE DIP
TURNIP TRUFFLE TRIPLE FLIP
GARLIC GUMBO GRAVY GUAVA
LENTIL LEMON LIVER LAVA
ORANGE OLIVE BAGEL BEET
WATERMELON WAFFLE WHEAT

I am Ebenezer Bleezer,
I run BLEEZER'S ICE-CREAM STORE,
taste a flavour from my freezer,
you will surely ask for more.

JACK PRELUTSKY

48

THE REMARKABLE CAKE

It's Christmas – the time when we gather to make
A truly remarkable once-a-year cake.
The recipe's written in letters of gold
By a family witch who is terribly old.

The rule of this cake is it has to be made
In a wheelbarrow (stirred with a shovel or spade)
At Christmas, the season of love and good will.
Other times of the year it might make you feel ill.

You must nail it together or stick it with glue,
Then hammer it flat with the heel of your shoe.
You must stretch it out thin, you must tie it in knots,
Then get out your paint box and paint it with spots.

What a taste! What a flavour! It's certain to please.
It's rather like ice-cream with pickles and cheese.
In June it would taste like spaghetti and mud,
While its taste in September would curdle your
  blood.

Oh, what a cake! It looks simply delicious.
Now get out the carving knife, get out the dishes!
Be careful! Be careful! This cake might explode,
And blow up the kitchen and part of the road.

Oh dear! It's exploded! I thought that it might.
It's not very often we get it just right.
Let's comfort the baby, revive Uncle Dan,
And we'll start it all over as soon as we can.

For Christmas – that gipsy day – comes and it goes
Far sooner than ever we dare to suppose.
Once more in December we'll gather to make
That truly remarkable once-a-year cake.

MARGARET MAHY

'I'VE EATEN MANY STRANGE AND SCRUMPTIOUS DISHES . . .'

'I've eaten many strange and scrumptious dishes in
   my time,
Like jellied gnats and dandyprats and earwigs cooked
   in slime,
And mice with rice – they're really nice
When roasted in their prime.
(But don't forget to sprinkle them with just a pinch
   of grime.)

'I've eaten fresh mudburgers by the greatest cooks
   there are,
And scrambled dregs and stinkbugs' eggs and
   hornets stewed in tar,
And pails of snails and lizards' tails,
And beetles by the jar.
(A beetle is improved by just a splash of vinegar.)

'I often eat boiled slobbages. They're grand when
    served beside
Minced doodlebugs and curried slugs. And have you
    ever tried
Mosquitoes' toes and wampfish roes
Most delicately fried?
(The only trouble is they disagree with my inside.)

'I'm mad for crispy wasp-stings on a piece of
    buttered toast,
And pickled spines of porcupines. And then a
    gorgeous roast
Of dragon's flesh, well hung, not fresh –
It costs a pound at most,
(And comes to you in barrels if you order it by post.)

'I crave the tasty tentacles of octopi for tea
I like hot-dogs, I LOVE hot-frogs, and surely you'll
    agree
A plate of soil with engine oil's
A super recipe.
(I hardly need to mention that it's practically free.)

'For dinner on my birthday shall I tell you what I
    chose:
Hot noodles made from poodles on a slice of garden
    hose –
And a rather smelly jelly
Made of armadillo's toes.
(The jelly is delicious, but you have to hold your nose.)

'Now comes,' *the Centipede declared*, 'the burden of my
    speech:
These foods are rare beyond compare – some are
    right out of reach;
But there's no doubt I'd go without
A million plates of each
For one small mite,
One tiny bite
Of this FANTASTIC PEACH!'

ROALD DAHL

BROTHER AND SISTER

'Sister, sister, go to bed,
Go and rest your weary head,'
Thus the prudent brother said.

'Do you want a battered hide
Or scratches to your face applied?'
Thus the sister calm replied.

'Sister! do not rouse my wrath,
I'd make you into mutton broth
As easily as kill a moth.'

The sister raised her beaming eye,
And looked on him indignantly,
And sternly answered 'Only try!'

Off to the cook he quickly ran,
'Dear cook, pray lend a frying pan
To me, as quickly as you can.'

'And wherefore should I give it you?'
'The reason, cook, is plain to view,
I wish to make an Irish stew.'

'What meat is in that stew to go?'
'My sister'll be the contents.' 'Oh!'
'Will you lend the pan, cook?' 'NO!'

MORAL
'Never stew your sister.'

LEWIS CARROLL

You Must Never Bath in an Irish Stew

You must never bath in an Irish Stew
It's a most illogical thing to do
    But should you persist against my reasoning
    Don't fail to add the appropriate seasoning.

SPIKE MILLIGAN

THE FRIENDLY CINNAMON BUN

Shining in his stickiness and glistening with honey,
Safe among his sisters and his brothers on a tray,
With raisin eyes that looked at me as I put down my
  money,
There smiled a friendly cinnamon bun, and this I
  heard him say:

'It's a lovely, lovely morning, and the world's a lovely
  place;
I know it's going to be a lovely day.
I know we're going to be good friends; I like your
  honest face;
Together we might go a long, long way.'

The baker's girl rang up the sale, 'I'll wrap your
  bun,' said she.
'Oh no, you needn't bother,' I replied.
I smiled back at that cinnamon bun and ate him, one
  two three,
And walked out with his friendliness inside.

                                    RUSSELL HOBAN

BUTTONS

There was an old skinflint of Hitching
Had a cook, Mrs Casey, of Cork;
There was nothing but crusts in the kitchen,
While in parlour was sherry and pork.
So at last, Mrs Casey, her pangs to assuage,
Having snipped off his buttonses, curried the page;
And now, while that skinflint gulps sherry and pork
In his parlour adjacent to Hitching,
To the tune blithe and merry of knife and of fork,
Anthropophagy reigns in the kitchen.

WALTER DE LA MARE

58

The sun was shining on the sea
   Shining with all his might:
He did his very best to make
   The billows smooth and bright –
And this was odd, because it was
   The middle of the night.

The moon was shining sulkily,
   Because she thought the sun
Had got no business to be there
   After the day was done –
'It's very rude of him,' she said,
   'To come and spoil the fun!'

The sea was wet as wet could be,
   The sands were dry as dry.
You could not see a cloud, because
   No cloud was in the sky:
No birds were flying overhead –
   There were no birds to fly.

The Walrus and the Carpenter
  Were walking close at hand;
They wept like anything to see
  Such quantities of sand:
'If this were only cleared away,'
  They said, 'it *would* be grand!'

'If seven maids with seven mops
  Swept it for half a year,
Do you suppose,' the Walrus said,
  'That they could get it clear?'
'I doubt it,' said the Carpenter,
  And shed a bitter tear.

'O Oysters, come and walk with us!'
  The Walrus did beseech.
'A pleasant walk, a pleasant talk,
  Along the briny beach:
We cannot do with more than four,
  To give a hand to each.'

The eldest Oyster looked at him,
　　But never a word he said:
The eldest Oyster winked his eye,
　　And shook his heavy head –
Meaning to say he did not choose
　　To leave the oyster-bed.

But four young Oysters hurried up,
　　All eager for the treat:
Their coats were brushed, their faces washed,
　　Their shoes were clean and neat –
And this was odd, because, you know,
　　They hadn't any feet.

Four other Oysters followed them,
　　And yet another four;
And thick and fast they came at last,
　　And more, and more, and more –
All hopping through the frothy waves,
　　And scrambling to the shore.

The Walrus and the Carpenter
    Walked on a mile or so.
And then they rested on a rock
    Conveniently low:
And all the little Oysters stood
    And waited in a row.

'The time has come,' the Walrus said,
   'To talk of many things:
Of shoes – and ships – and sealing-wax –
   Of cabbages – and kings –
And why the sea is boiling hot –
   And whether pigs have wings.'

'But wait a bit,' the Oysters cried,
   'Before we have our chat;
For some of us are out of breath,
   And all of us are fat!'
'No hurry!' said the Carpenter.
   They thanked him much for that.

'A loaf of bread,' the Walrus said,
    'Is what we chiefly need:
Pepper and vinegar besides
    Are very good indeed –
Now if you're ready, Oysters dear,
    We can begin to feed.'

'But not on us!' the Oysters cried,
    Turning a little blue.
'After such kindness, that would be
    A dismal thing to do!'
'The night is fine,' the Walrus said.
    'Do you admire the view?'

'It was so kind of you to come!
    And you are very nice!'
The Carpenter said nothing but
    'Cut us another slice:
I wish you were not quite so deaf –
    I've had to ask you twice!'

'It seems a shame,' the Walrus said,
    'To play them such a trick,
After we've brought them out so far,
    And made them trot so quick!'
The Carpenter said nothing but
    'The butter's spread too thick!'

'I weep for you,' the Walrus said:
    'I deeply sympathize.'
With sobs and tears he sorted out
    Those of the largest size,
Holding his pocket-handkerchief
    Before his streaming eyes.

'O Oysters,' said the Carpenter,
    'You've had a pleasant run!
Shall we be trotting home again?'
    But answer came there none –
And this was scarcely odd, because
    They'd eaten every one.

                    LEWIS CARROLL

MINNOW MINNIE

May I ask you if you've noticed,
May I ask you if you've seen
My minnow Minnie
Who was swimmin'
In your Ovaltine?
For you've gone and drunk it up, dear,
And she isn't in the cup, dear,
And she's nowhere to be found, dear.
Do you think that she has drowned, dear?

SHEL SILVERSTEIN

FAME WAS A CLAIM OF UNCLE ED'S

Fame was a claim of Uncle Ed's,
Simply because he had three heads,
Which, if he'd only had a third of,
I think he would never have been heard of.

OGDEN NASH

from *MELODIES*

There was once a young man of Oporta
Who daily got shorter and shorter,
   The reason he said
   Was the hod on his head,
Which was filled with the *heaviest* mortar.

His sister named Lucy O'Finner,
Grew constantly thinner and thinner,
   The reason was plain,
   She slept out in the rain,
And was never allowed any dinner.

LEWIS CARROLL

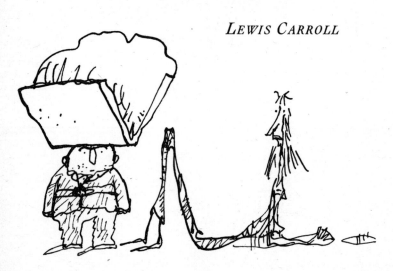

THERE WAS AN OLD PERSON OF SLOUGH

There was an Old Person of Slough,
who danced at the end of a Bough;
But they said, 'If you sneeze,
you might damage the trees,
You imprudent Old Person of Slough.'

EDWARD LEAR

INCIDENTS IN THE LIFE OF MY UNCLE ARLEY

[I]

O my agèd Uncle Arly!
Sitting on a heap of Barley
    Thro' the silent hours of night, –
Close beside a leafy thicket: –
On his nose there was a Cricket, –
In his hat a Railway-Ticket; –
    (But his shoes were far too tight.)

[II]

Long ago, in youth, he squander'd
All his goods away, and wander'd
    To the Tiniskoop-hills afar.
There on golden sunsets blazing,
Every evening found him gazing, –
Singing, – 'Orb! you're quite amazing!
    How I wonder what you are!'

[III]

Like the ancient Medes and Persians,
Always by his own exertions
 He subsisted on those hills; –
Whiles, – by teaching children spelling, –
Or at times by merely yelling, –
Or at intervals by selling
 Propter's Nicodemus Pills.

[IV]

Later, in his morning rambles
He perceived the moving brambles –
 Something square and white disclose; –
'Twas a First-class Railway-Ticket;
But, on stooping down to pick it
Off the ground, – a pea-green Cricket
 Settled on my uncle's Nose.

[V]

Never – never more, – oh! never,
Did that Cricket leave him ever, –
    Dawn or evening, day or night; –
Clinging as a constant treasure, –
Chirping with a cheerious measure, –
Wholly to my uncle's pleasure, –
    (Though his shoes were far too tight.)

[VI]

So for three-and-forty winters,
Till his shoes were worn to splinters,
    All those hills he wander'd o'er, –
Sometimes silent; – sometimes yelling; –
Till he came to Borley-Melling,
Near his old ancestral dwelling; –
    (But his shoes were far too tight.)

[VII]

On a little heap of Barley
Died my agèd uncle Arly,
    And they buried him one night; –
Close beside the leafy thicket; –
There, – his hat and Railway-Ticket; –
There, – his ever-faithful Cricket; –
    (But his shoes were far too tight.)

EDWARD LEAR

THERE WAS AN OLD PERSON IN GRAY

There was an Old Person in Gray,
whose feelings were tinged with dismay;
She purchased two Parrots,
and fed them with Carrots,
Which pleased that Old Person in Gray.

EDWARD LEAR

MOONSHINE

There was a young lady of Rheims,
   There was an old poet of Gizeh;
He rhymed on the deepest and sweetest of themes,
   She scorned all his efforts to please her:
         And he sighed, 'Ah, I see,
         She and sense won't agree.'
So he scribbled her moonshine, mere moonshine,
   and she,
With jubilant screams, packed her trunk up in
   Rheims,
Cried aloud, 'I am coming, O Bard of my dreams!'
   And was clasped to his bosom in Gizeh.

WALTER DE LA MARE

JERRY HALL

Jerry Hall
Is so small,
A rat could eat him
Hat and all.

ANONYMOUS

SOME AUNTS AND UNCLES

When Aunty Jane
Became a Crane
She put one leg behind her head;
And even when the clock struck ten
Refused to go to bed.

When Aunty Grace
Became a Plaice
She all but vanished sideways on;
Except her nose
And pointed toes
The rest of her was gone.

When Aunty Flo
Became a Crow
She had a bed put in a tree;
And there she lay
And read all day
Of ornithology.

When Aunty Vi
Became a Fly
Her favourite nephew
Sought her life;
How could he know
That with each blow
He bruised his Uncle's wife?

When Aunty Mig
Became a Pig
She floated on the briny breeze,
With irritation in her heart
And warts upon her knees.

When Uncle Jake
Became a Snake
He never found it out;
And so as no one mentions it
One sees him still about.

MERVYN PEAKE

MRS MCPHEE

Mrs McPhee
Who lived in South Zeal
Roasted a duckling
For every meal.

'Duckling for breakfast
And dinner and tea,
And duckling for supper,'
Said Mrs McPhee.

'It's sweeter than sugar,
It's clean as a nut,
I'm sure and I'm certain
It's good for me – BUT

'I don't like these feathers
That grow on my back,
And my silly webbed feet
And my voice that goes quack.'

As easy and soft
As a ship to the sea,
As a duck to the water
Went Mrs McPhee.

'I think I'll go swim
In the river,' said she;
Said Mrs Mac, Mrs Quack,
Mrs McPhee.

CHARLES CAUSLEY

THERE WAS A MAD MAN

There was a Mad Man,
And he had a Mad Wife,
And they lived in a Mad town,
They had three Children
All at a Birth,
And they were Mad
Every One.

The Father was Mad,
The Mother was Mad,
The Children all Mad besides,
And they all got
Upon a Mad Horse,
And Madly they did ride.

They rode by night and they rode by day,
Yet never a one of them fell,
They rode so madly all the way,
Till they came to the gates of hell.

Old Nick was glad to see them so mad,
And gladly let them in:
But he soon grew sorry to see him so merry,
And let them out again.

ANONYMOUS

A FRIEND TO THE CHILDREN

THE YAK

As a friend to the children
>> commend me the Yak.
> You will find it exactly the thing:
It will carry and fetch,
>> you can ride on its back,
Or lead it about
>> with a string.
The Tartar who dwells on the plains of Thibet
> (A desolate region of snow)
Has for centuries made it a nursery pet,
> And surely the Tartar should know!
Then tell your papa where the Yak can be got
> And if he is awfully rich
He will buy you the creature –
>> or else
>> he will *not*.
(I cannot be positive which.)

HILAIRE BELLOC

A SUNNIT TO THE BIG OX

*(Composed while standing within two feet of him, and a
tuchin' of him now and then.)*

————————

All hale! thou mighty annimil – all hale!
You are 4 thousand pounds, and am purty wel
Perporshund, thou tremendjus boveen nuggit!
I wonder how big yu was when yu
Was little, and if yure mother would no yu now
That yu've grone so long, and thick and fat;
Or if yure father would rekognise his ofspring
And his kaff, thou elephanteen quadrupid!
I wonder if it hurts yu much to be so big,
And if yu grode it in a month or so.
I spose wen yu was young tha didn't gin
Yu skim milk but all the creme yu could stuff
Into yore little stummick, jest to see
How big yu'd gro; and afterward tha no doubt
Fed yu on oats and hay and sich like,
With perhaps an occasional punkin or squosh!
In all probability yu don't know yure anny
Bigger than a small kaff; for if yu did
Yude break down fences and switch yure tail,

And rush around and hook and beller,
And run over fowkes, thou orful beast.
O, what a lot of mince pies yude maik,
And sassengers, and your tail,
Whitch can't weigh fur from forty pounds,
Wud maik nigh unto a barrel of ox-tail soup,
And cudn't a heep of staiks be cut off you,
Whitch, with salt and pepper and termater
Ketchup, wouldn't be bad to taik.
Thou grate and glorious inseckt!
But I must close, O most prodijus reptile!
And for mi admiration of yu, when yu di,
I'le rite a node unto yure peddy and remanes,
Pernouncin yu the largest of yure race;
And as I don't expec to have half a dollar
Again to spair for to pay to look at yu, and as
I ain't a dead head, I will sa, farewell.

ANONYMOUS

THE ELEPHANT OR, THE FORCE OF HABIT

A tail behind, a trunk in front,
Complete the usual elephant.
The tail in front, the trunk behind
Is what you very seldom find.

If you for specimens should hunt
With trunks behind and tails in front,
That hunt would occupy you long;
The force of habit is so strong.

A. E. HOUSMAN

ELETELEPHONY

Once there was an elephant,
Who tried to use the telephant –
No! no! I mean an elephone
Who tried to use the telephone –
(Dear me! I am not certain quite
That even now I've got it right.)

Howe'er it was, he got his trunk
Entangled in the telephunk;
The more he tried to get it free,
The louder buzzed the telephee –
(I fear I'd better drop the song
Of elephop and telephong!)

LAURA RICHARDS

from THE CROCODILE OR, PUBLIC DECENCY

Though some at my aversion smile,
I cannot love the crocodile.
Its conduct does not seem to me
Consistent with sincerity.

Where Nile, with beneficial flood,
Improves the desert sand to mud,
The infant child, its banks upon,
Will run about with nothing on.
The London County Council not
Being adjacent to the spot,
This is the consequence. Meanwhile,
What is that object in the Nile
Which swallows water, chokes and spits?
It is the crocodile in fits.

'Oh infant! oh my country's shame!
Suppose a European came!
Picture his feelings, on his pure
Personally conducted tour!
The British Peer's averted look,
The mantling blush of Messrs Cook!
Come, awful infant, come and be
Dressed, if in nothing else, in me.'

Then disappears into the Nile
The infant, clad in crocodile,
And meekly yields his youthful breath
To darkness, decency, and death.
His mother, in the local dells,
Deplores him with Egyptian yells:
Her hieroglyphic howls are vain,
Nor will the lost return again.
The crocodile itself no less
Displays, but does not feel, distress,

And with its tears augments the Nile;
The false, amphibious crocodile.

A. E. HOUSMAN

THE PURIST

I give you now Professor Twist,
A conscientious scientist,
Trustees exclaimed, 'He never bungles!'
And sent him off to distant jungles.
Camped on a tropic riverside,
One day he missed his loving bride.
She had, the guide informed him later,
Been eaten by an alligator.
Professor Twist could not but smile.
'You mean,' he said, 'a crocodile.'

OGDEN NASH

SOME VERSES TO SNAIX

Prodiggus reptile! long and skaly kuss!
You are the dadrattedest biggest thing I ever
Seed that cud ty itself into a double bo-
Not, and cum all strate again in a
Minnit or so, without winkin or seemin
To experience any particular pane
In the diafram.

Stoopenjus inseck! marvelous annimile!
You are no doubt seven thousand yeres
Old, and hav a considerable of a
Family sneekin round thru the tall
Gras in Africa, a eetin up little greezy
Piggers, and wishin they was biggir.

I wonder how big yu was when yu
Was a inphant about 2 fete long. I
Expec yu was a purty good size, and
Lived on phrogs, and lizzerds, and polly-
Wogs and sutch things.

You are havin' a nice time now, ennyhow –
Don't have nothing to do but lay oph.
And ete kats and rabbits, and stic
Out yure tung and twist yur tale.
I wunder if yu ever swollered a man
Without takin oph his butes. If there was
Brass buttins on his kote, I spose

Yu had ter swaller a lot of buttin-
Wholes, and a shu-hamer to nock
The soals oph of the boots and drive in
The tax, so that they would n't kut yure
Inside. I wunder if vittles taste
Good all the way down. I expec so –
At leest, fur 6 or 7 fete.

You are so mighty long, I shud thynk
If your tale was kold, yure hed
Woodent no it till the next day,
But it's hard tu tell: snaix is snaix.

ANONYMOUS

S F

———

From my city bed in the dawn I
    see a raccoon
On my neighbour's roof.
He walks along in his wisdom in the
    gutter,
And passes from view
On his way to his striped
    spaceship to doff his disguise
And return to Mars
As a Martian
Raccoon.

ERNEST LEVERETT

THE MAD HATTER'S SONG

Twinkle, twinkle, little bat!
How I wonder what you're at!
Up above the world you fly,
Like a tea-tray in the sky.
                Twinkle, twinkle –

LEWIS CARROLL

THE DEDICATED TRAVELLER

ANFRUCA
(AN-FROO'KA)

—————

When I go to Anfruca (which is very, very far –
too far for a bicycle, too far for a car)
I always take a bucket and I always take a spade,
for we may be gathering sponges and we may be
   digging jade
in Anfruca where I go
(near the crow).

In Anfruca there are oogans and they live among the
   trees,
and some of them are all of them; they do just as they
   please.
They wheel their wheelbarrows in the wheelbarrow
   races
and they always carry bookmarks so they never lose
   their places
in Anfruca where I go
(near the crow).

That's where Charlie Everybody and his brother
  spend the summer
with a lightning bug to read by and a bullfrog for a
  drummer.
They march with all the oogans when they do
  Anfrucan walking
and they spell out words in pebbles so the crow
  won't hear them talking
in Anfruca where I go
(near the crow).

Do you know how the crow
always knows
when he goes
to his house how to go?
Well, he knows he must go
through Anfruca (fast or slow)
till he sees the name of Crow.
Now you know.

RUSSELL HOBAN

THE OWL AND THE PUSSY-CAT

[1]

The Owl and the Pussy-cat went to sea
  In a beautiful pea-green boat,
They took some honey, and plenty of money,
  Wrapped up in a five-pound note.
The Owl looked up to the stars above,
  And sang to a small guitar,
'O lovely Pussy! O Pussy, my love,
    What a beautiful Pussy you are,
        You are,
        You are!
What a beautiful Pussy you are!'

[II]

Pussy said to the Owl, 'You elegant fowl!
   How charmingly sweet you sing!
O let us be married! too long we have tarried:
   But what shall we do for a ring?'
They sailed away, for a year and a day,
   To the land where the Bong-tree grows
And there in a wood a Piggy-wig stood
     With a ring at the end of his nose,
       His nose,
       His nose,
   With a ring at the end of his nose.

'Dear Pig, are you willing to sell for one shilling
   Your ring?' Said the Piggy, 'I will.'
So they took it away, and were married next day
   By the Turkey who lives on the hill.
They dined on mince, and slices of quince,
   Which they ate with a runcible spoon;
And hand in hand, on the edge of the sand,
      They danced by the light of the moon,
         The moon,
         The moon,
They danced by the light of the moon.

EDWARD LEAR

THE ISLAND OF LLINCE

The island of Llince
is covered in chintz
printed in patterns
of rhubarb and quince.
The King who once lived there
has not been seen since
they wrapped up his kingdom
in fathoms of chintz.

N. M. BODECKER

ON THE NING NANG NONG

On the Ning Nang Nong
Where the Cows go Bong!
And the Monkeys all say Boo!
There's a Nong Nang Ning
Where the trees go Ping!
And the tea-pots Jibber Jabber Joo.
On the Nong Ning Nang
All the mice go Clang!
And you just can't catch 'em when they do!
So it's Ning Nang Nong!
Cows go Bong!
Nong Nang Ning!
Trees go Ping!
Nong Ning Nang!
The mice go Clang!
What a noisy place to belong,
Is the Ning Nang Ning Nang Nong!!

SPIKE MILLIGAN

THE JUMBLES

[1]

They went to sea in a Sieve, they did,
  In a Sieve they went to sea:
In spite of all their friends could say,
On a winter's morn, on a stormy day,
  In a Sieve they went to sea!
And when the Sieve turned round and round,
And every one cried, 'You'll all be drowned!'
They called aloud, 'Our Sieve ain't big,
But we don't care a button! we don't care a fig!
  In a Sieve we'll go to sea!'
    Far and few, far and few,
      Are the lands where the Jumblies live;
      Their heads are green, and their hands are blue,
      And they went to sea in a Sieve.

[II]

They sailed in a Sieve, they did,
   In a Sieve they sailed so fast,
With only a beautiful pea-green veil
Tied with a riband by way of a sail,
   To a small tobacco-pipe mast;
And every one said, who saw them go,
'O won't they be soon upset, you know!
For the sky is dark, and the voyage is long,
And happen what may, it's extremely wrong
   In a Sieve to sail so fast!'
      Far and few, far and few,
         Are the lands where the Jumblies live;
      Their heads are green, and their hands are blue,
         And they went to sea in a Sieve.

The water it soon came in, it did,
  The water it soon came in;
So to keep them dry, they wrapped their feet
In a pinky paper all folded neat,
  And they fastened it down with a pin.
And they passed the night in a crockery-jar,
And each of them said, 'How wise we are!
Though the sky be dark, and the voyage be long,
Yet we never can think we were rash or wrong,
  While round in our Sieve we spin!'
    Far and few, far and few,
      Are the lands where the Jumblies live;
      Their heads are green, and their hands are blue,
      And they went to sea in a Sieve.

[IV]

And all night long they sailed away;
  And when the sun went down,
They whistled and warbled a moony song
To the echoing sound of a coppery gong,
  In the shade of the mountains brown.
'O Timballo! How happy we are,
When we live in a sieve and a crockery-jar,
And all night long in the moonlight pale,
We sail away with a pea-green sail,
  In the shade of the mountains brown!'
    Far and few, far and few,
      Are the lands where the Jumblies live;
      Their heads are green, and their hands are blue,
        And they went to sea in a Sieve.

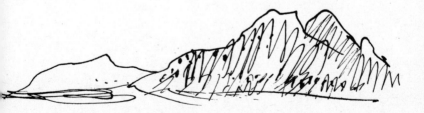

[v]

They sailed to the Western Sea, they did,
   To a land all covered with trees,
And they bought an Owl, and a useful Cart,
And a pound of Rice, and a Cranberry Tart,
   And a hive of silvery Bees.
And they bought a Pig, and some green Jack-daws,
And a lovely Monkey with lollipop paws,
And forty bottles of Ring-Bo-Ree,
   And no end of Stilton Cheese.
    Far and few, far and few,
      Are the lands where the Jumblies live;
     Their heads are green, and their hands are blue,
     And they went to sea in a Sieve.

[VI]

And in twenty years they all came back,
  In twenty years or more,
And every one said, 'How tall they've grown!
For they've been to the Lakes, and the Torrible
  Zone,
  And the hills of the Chankly Bore';
And they drank their health, and gave them a feast
Of dumplings made of beautiful yeast;
And every one said, 'If we only live,
We too will go to sea in a Sieve, –
  To the hills of the Chankly Bore!'
    Far and few, far and few,
      Are the lands where the Jumblies live;
    Their heads are green, and their hands are blue,
      And they went to sea in a Sieve.

EDWARD LEAR

HOW I BROUGHT THE GOOD NEWS
FROM AIX TO GHENT OR, VICE VERSA

I sprang to the rollocks and Jorrocks and me,
And I galloped, you galloped, we galloped all three.
Not a word to each other: we kept changing place,
Neck to neck, back to front, ear to ear, face to face:
And we yelled once or twice, when we heard a clock
  chime,
'Would you kindly oblige us, *is that the right time?*'
As I galloped, you galloped, he galloped, we
  galloped, ye galloped, they two shall have
  galloped: *let us trot*.

I unsaddled the saddle, unbuckled the bit,
Unshackled the bridle (the thing didn't fit)
And ungalloped, ungalloped, ungalloped, ungalloped
  a bit.
Then I cast off my buff coat, let my bowler hat fall,
Took off both my boots and my trousers and all –
Drank off my stirrup-cup, felt a bit tight,
And unbridled the saddle: it still wasn't right.

Then all I remember is, things reeling round,
As I sat with my head 'twixt my ears on the ground –
For imagine my shame when they asked what I
  meant
And I had to confess that I'd been, gone and went
And *forgotten* the news I was bringing to Ghent,
Though I'd galloped and galloped and galloped and
  galloped and galloped
And galloped and galloped and galloped. (Had I not
  would have been galloped?)

Envoi

So I sprang to a taxi and shouted 'To Aix!'
And he blew on his horn and he threw off his brakes,
And all the way back till my money was spent
We rattled and rattled and rattled and rattled and
  rattled
And rattled and rattled –
And eventually sent a telegram.

W. C. SELLAR AND R. J. YEATMAN

THE NUTCRACKERS AND THE SUGAR-TONGS

[I]

The Nutcrackers sate by a plate on the table,
  The Sugar-tongs sate by a plate at his side;
And the Nutcrackers said, 'Don't you wish we were able
  'Along the blue hills and green meadows to ride?
'Must we drag on this stupid existence for ever,
  'So idle and weary, so full of remorse, –
'While every one else takes his pleasure, and never
  'Seems happy unless he is riding a horse?

[II]

'Don't you think we could ride without being instructed?
  'Without any saddle, or bridle, or spur?
'Our legs are so long, and so aptly constructed,
  'I'm sure that an accident could not occur.
'Let us all of a sudden hop down from the table,
  'And hustle downstairs, and each jump on a horse!

'Shall we try? Shall we go? Do you think we are
    able?'
    The Sugar-tongs answered distinctly, 'Of course!'

[III]
So down the long staircase they hopped in a minute,
    The Sugar-tongs snapped, and the Crackers said
    'crack!'
The stable was open, the horses were in it;
    Each took out a pony, and jumped on his back.
The Cat in a fright scrambled out of the doorway,
    The Mice tumbled out of a bundle of hay,
The brown and white Rats, and the black ones
    from Norway,
    Screamed out, 'They are taking the horses away!'

[IV]
The whole of the household was filled with
    amazement,
    The Cups and the Saucers danced madly about,
The Plates and the Dishes looked out of the
    casement,
    The Saltcellar stood on his head with a shout,

The Spoons with a clatter looked out of the lattice,
   The Mustard-pot climbed up the Gooseberry Pies,
The Soup-ladle peeped through a heap of Veal
   Patties,
   And squeaked with a ladle-like scream of surprise.

[v]

The Frying-pan said, 'It's an awful delusion!'
   The Tea-kettle hissed and grew black in the face;
And they all rushed downstairs in the wildest
   confusion,
   To see the great Nutcracker-Sugar-tong race.
And out of the stable, with screamings and laughter,
   (Their ponies were cream-coloured, speckled with
   brown,)
The Nutcrackers first, and the Sugar-tongs after,
   Rode all round the yard, and then all round the
   town.

[VI]

They rode through the street, and they rode by the
    station,
    They galloped away to the beautiful shore;
In silence they rode, and 'made no observation',
    Save this: 'We will never go back any more!'
And still you might hear, till they rode out of
    hearing,
    The Sugar-tongs snap, and the Crackers say
    'crack!'
Till far in the distance their forms disappearing,
They faded away – and they never came back!

Edward Lear

119

THE ROAD TO ZOAGLI
(*Ligurian Folk Song*)

───────

Have ye seen the would-be-not-humble dandy,
 With his long black cloak and his short trousers
grey?
I saw him, dear heart, this morn as ever was, on the
                                    road to Zoagli,
 And I looked the other way.

What said the would-be-not-humble dandy,
    With his long black cloak and his short trousers
    grey?'
He said naught, dear heart, this morn as ever was,
    on the

                                    road to Zoagli,
    And I looked the other way.

How fared the would-be-not-humble dandy,
    With his long black cloak and his short trousers
    grey?
He fared ill, dear heart, this morn as ever was, on the
                                    road to Zoagli,
    For dead he lay.

                                    Max Beerbohm

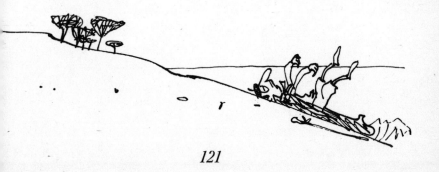

O'er Seas That Have No Beaches

O'er seas that have no beaches
To end their waves upon,
I floated with twelve peaches,
A sofa and a swan.

The blunt waves crashed above us
The sharp waves burst around,
There was no one to love us,
No hope of being found –

Where, on the notched horizon
So endlessly a-drip,
I saw all of a sudden
No sign of any ship.

MERVYN PEAKE

THE BONGALOO AND THE SCRUNCH

A QUADRUPEDREMIAN SONG

He dreamt that he saw the Buffalant,
   And the spottified Dromedaraffe,
The blue Camelotamus, lean and gaunt,
   And the wild Tigeroceros calf.

The maned Liodillo loudly roared,
   And the Peccarbok whistled its whine,
The Chinchayak leapt on the dewy sward,
   As it hunted the pale Baboopine.

He dreamt that he met the Crocoghau,
   As it swam in the Stagnolent Lake;
But everything that in dreams he saw
   Came of eating too freely of cake.

THOMAS HOOD THE YOUNGER

THE WENDIGO

The Wendigo,
The Wendigo!
Its eyes are ice and indigo!
Its blood is rank and yellowish!
Its voice is hoarse and bellowish!
Its tentacles are slithery,
And scummy,
Slimy,
Leathery!
Its lips are hungry blubbery,
And smacky,
Sucky,
Rubbery!

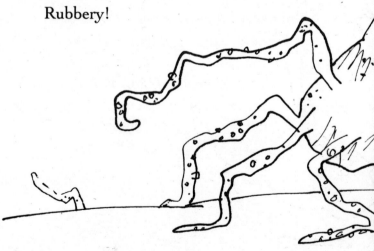

The Wendigo,
The Wendigo!
I saw it just a friend ago!
Last night it lurked in Canada;
Tonight, on your veranada!
As you are lolling hammockwise
It contemplates you stomachwise.
You loll,
It contemplates,
It lollops.
The rest is merely gulps and gollops.

OGDEN NASH

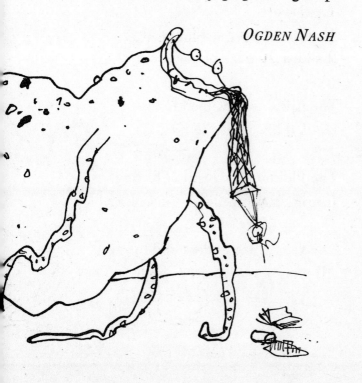

THE UTTER ZOO ALPHABET

The Ampoo is intensely neat;
Its head is small, likewise its feet.

The Boggerslosh conceals itself
In back of bottles on a shelf.

The Crunk is not unseldom drastic
And must be hindered by elastic.

The Dawbis is remote and shy;
It shuns the gaze of passers-by.

The Epitwee's inclined to fits
Until at last it falls to bits.

The Fidknop is devoid of feeling;
It drifts about beneath the ceiling.

The Gawdge is understood to save
All sorts of objects in its cave.

The Humglum crawls along the ground
And never makes the slightest sound.

The Ippagoggy has a taste
For every kind of glue and paste.

The Jelbislup cannot get far
Because it's kept inside a jar.

The Kwongdzu has enormous claws;
Its character is full of flaws.

The Limplig finds it hard to keep
From spending all its life asleep.

The Mork proceeds with pensive grace
And no expression on its face.

The Neapse's sufferings are chronic;
It lives exclusively on tonic.

The Ombledroom is vast and white
And therefore visible by night.

The Posby goes into a trance
In which it does a little dance.

The Quingawaga squeaks and moans
While dining off of ankle bones.

The Raitch hangs downward from its tail
By knotting it around a nail.

The Scrug's extremely nasty-looking
And is unusable for cooking.

The Twibbit on occasion knows
A difficulty with its toes.

The Ulp is very, very small;
It hardly can be seen at all.

The Veazy makes a creaking noise;
It has no dignity or poise.

The Wambulus has floppy ears
With which it wipes away its tears.

The Xyke stands up at close of day,
And then it slowly walks away.

The Yawfle stares, and stares, and stares.
And stares, and stares, and stares, and stares.

About the Zote what can be said?
There was just one, and now it's dead.

EDWARD GOREY

THE BLUNDERBLAT

———————

Until I saw the Blunderblat
I doubted its existence;
But late last night with Vera White,
I saw one in the distance.

I reached for my binoculars,
Which finally I focused;
I watched it rise into the skies,
Like some colossal locust.

I heard it hover overhead,
I shrieked as it came nearer;
I held my breath, half scared to death,
And prayed it might take Vera.

And so it did, I'm glad to say,
Without too much resistance.
Dear Blunderblat, I'm sorry that
I doubted your existence.

COLIN WEST

THE BONGALOO

'What is a Bongaloo, Daddy?'
'A Bongaloo, Son,' said I,
'Is a tall bag of cheese
Plus a Chinaman's knees
And the leg of a nanny goat's eye.'

'How strange is a Bongaloo, Daddy?'
'As strange as strange,' I replied.
'When the sun's in the West
It appears in a vest
Sailing out with the noonday tide.'

'What shape is a Bongaloo, Daddy?'
'The shape, my Son, I'll explain:
It's tall round the nose
Which continually grows
In the general direction of Spain.'

'Are you *sure* there's a Bongaloo, Daddy?'
'Am I sure, my Son?' said I.
'Why, I've seen it, not quite
On a dark sunny night
Do you think that I'd tell you a lie?'

SPIKE MILLIGAN

134

'THERE IS NO KNOWING WHAT WE SHALL SEE!' . . .

'There is no knowing what we shall see!' cried the
  Centipede.

'We may see a Creature with forty-nine heads
Who lives in the desolate snow,
And whenever he catches a cold (which he dreads)
He has forty-nine noses to blow.

'We may see the venomous Pink-Spotted Scrunch
Who can chew up a man with one bite.
It likes to eat five of them roasted for lunch
And eighteen for its supper at night.

'We may see a Dragon, and nobody knows
That we won't see a Unicorn there.
We may see a terrible Monster with toes
Growing out of the tufts of his hair.

'We may see the sweet little Biddy-Bright Hen
So playful, so kind and well-bred;
And such beautiful eggs! You just boil them and then
They explode and they blow off your head.

'A Gnu and a Gnocerous surely you'll see
And that gnormous and gnorrible Gnat
Whose sting when it stings you goes in at the knee
And comes out through the top of your hat.

'We may even get lost and be frozen by frost.
We may die in an earthquake or tremor.
Or nastier still, we may even be tossed
On the horns of a furious Dilemma.

'But who cares! Let us go from this horrible hill!
Let us roll! Let us bowl! Let us plunge!
Let's go rolling and bowling and spinning until
We're away from old Spiker and Sponge!'

ROALD DAHL

THE UNDERWATER WIBBLES

The Underwater Wibbles
dine exclusively on cheese,
they keep it in containers
which they bind about their knees,
they often chew on Cheddar
which they slice into a dish,
and gorge on Gorgonzola
to the wonder of the fish.

The Underwater Wibbles
wiggle blithely through the sea,
munching merrily on Muenster,
grated Feta, bits of Brie,
passing porpoises seem puzzled,
stolid octopuses stare,
as the Wibbles nibble Gouda,
Provolone, Camembert.

The Underwater Wibbles
frolic gaily off the coast,
eating melted Mozzarella
served on soggy crusts of toast,
Wibbles gobble Appenzeller
as they execute their dives,
oh, the Underwater Wibbles
live extraordinary lives.

JACK PRELUTSKY

THE WORST

When singing songs of scariness,
Of bloodiness and hairyness,
I feel obligated at this moment to remind you
Of the most ferocious beast of all:
Three thousand pounds and nine feet tall –
The Glurpy Slurpy Skakagrall –
Who's standing right behind you.

SHEL SILVERSTEIN

An Area of Uncertainty

A CHRONICLE

Once – but no matter when –
   There lived – no matter where –
A man, whose name – but then
   I need not that declare.

He – well, he had been born,
   And so he was alive;
His age – I details scorn –
   Was somethingty and five.

He lived – how many years
   I truly can't decide;
But this one fact appears
   He lived – until he died.

'He died,' I have averred,
   But cannot prove 't was so,
But that he was interred,
   At any rate, I know.

I fancy he'd a son,
  I hear he had a wife:
Perhaps he'd more than one,
  I know not, on my life!

But whether he was rich,
  Or whether he was poor,
Or neither – both – or which,
  I cannot say, I'm sure.

I can't recall his name,
  Or what he used to do:
But then – well, such is fame!
  'T will so serve me and you.

And that is why I thus,
  About this unknown man
Would fain create a fuss,
  To rescue, if I can.

From dark oblivion's blow,
    Some record of his lot:
But, ah! I do not know
    Who – where – when – why – or what.

MORAL

In this brief pedigree
    A moral we should find –
But what it ought to be
    Has quite escaped my mind!

ANONYMOUS

THERE'S A RATHER ODD COUPLE IN HERTS

There's a rather odd couple in Herts
Who are cousins (or so each asserts);
    Their sex is in doubt
    For they're never without
Their moustaches and long, trailing skirts.

EDWARD GOREY

INDIRECTIONS

The way to Upper Norwood, sir? Oh dear, oh dear,
  oh dear!
If that's where I was heading for, I wouldn't start
  from here.
But, since you seem determined and it's too late to
  turn back,
Just carry on until you see an ostrich in a sack;
Turn left, and cross the highway where the nuns are
  laying tar,
And then run up the gravelled hill. (You should have
  come by car.)

Once at the intersection you take any turn you like,
Except the fourteenth from the left. (You should
  have come by bike.)
Go carefully across the bridge – they've covered it in
  slime –
And throw your briefcase in the stream – it helps to
  pass the time;
You walk straight past the spotty youth with beetles
  on a tray,
And plunge into the nettle-bed. (You should have
  come by sleigh.)

Ahead of you you'll spot a group of sailors with their
  ship:
They'll ferry you across the road. (It's best to leave a
  tip.)

Then cross the patch of wasteland where the
   colonel's planting sheep
(They never come to anything: he buries them too
   deep);
Beyond the three archbishops playing cards and
   winding wool
You'll see, a little way in front, a vicious-looking bull.
Turn round and sprint for all you're worth. (You
   should have caught a train.)
That brings you back to where you are; then stop,
   and ask again.

JOHN YEOMAN

148

THE MAD GARDENER'S SONG

He thought he saw an Elephant,
   That practised on a fife:
He looked again, and found it was
   A letter from his wife.
'At length I realise,' he said,
   'The bitterness of Life!'

He thought he saw a Buffalo
   Upon the chimney-piece:
He looked again, and found it was
   His Sister's Husband's Niece.
'Unless you leave this house,' he said,
   'I'll send for the Police!'

He thought he saw a Rattlesnake
   That questioned him in Greek:
He looked again, and found it was
   The Middle of Next Week.
'The only thing I regret,' he said,
   'Is that it cannot speak!'

He thought he saw a Banker's Clerk
    Descending from the bus:
He looked again, and found it was
    A Hippopotamus:
'If this should stay to dine,' he said,
    'There won't be much for us!'

He thought he saw a Kangaroo
    That worked a coffee-mill:
He looked again, and found it was
    A Vegetable-Pill.
'Were I to swallow this,' he said,
    'I should be very ill!'

He thought he saw a Coach-and-Four
    That stood beside his bed:
He looked again, and found it was
    A Bear without a Head.
'Poor thing,' he said, 'poor silly thing!
    It's waiting to be fed!'

He thought he saw an Albatross
   That fluttered round the lamp:
He looked again, and found it was
   A Penny-Postage-Stamp.
'You'd best be getting home,' he said:
   'The nights are very damp!'

He thought he saw a Garden-Door
   That opened with a key:
He looked again, and found it was
   A Double Rule of Three:
'And all its mystery,' he said,
   'Is clear as day to me!'

He thought he saw an Argument
   That proved he was the Pope:
He looked again, and found it was
   A Bar of Mottled Soap.
'A fact so dread,' he faintly said,
   'Extinguishes all hope!'

LEWIS CARROLL

GAZEBOS

What I find wanting in gazebos
Is their herd instinct.
They either pose woodenly in clearings
Way off the beaten track
Or give us come hither looks
From across a grey smudge of lake.

And always alone. Aloof.
They can't even lay claim
To a collective noun. A posse?
A cluster? A conglomerate?
How they ever manage to reproduce
Is anybody's guess.

ROGER MCGOUGH

THE AMPHISBAENA OR, THE LIMITS OF HUMAN KNOWLEDGE

Amphisbaena: a serpent supposed to have two heads, and by consequence to move with either end foremost   *– Johnson*

If you should happen to descry
An Amphisbaena drawing nigh,
You may remain upon the spot,
But probably had better not.
The prudent its approach avoid
And do not stop to be annoyed,
For all who see it are perplexed
And wonder what will happen next.
Both ends, unfortunately, are
So singularly similar.
It has indeed a head in front
(As has the Indian elephant),
But then, to our alarm, we find
It has another head behind;
And hence zoologists affirm
That it is not a pachyderm.

Until it starts, you never know
In which direction it will go,
Nor can you even then maintain
That it will not come back again.
The sportsman, in amaze profound
Collapsing on his faithful hound,
Exclaims, as soon as he can speak,
'The Amphisbaena is unique.'
Unique no doubt it is; but oh,
That is not what distracts me so.
No: when before my musing eye
The Amphisbaena rambles by,
The question which bereaves of bliss

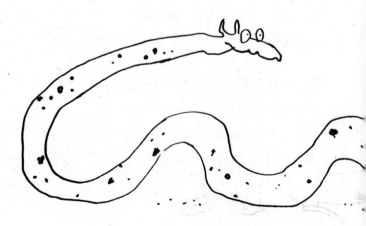

My finite intellect is this:
Who, who, oh, who will make it clear
Which is the front and which the rear?
Whether, at any given date,
The reptile is advancing straight,
Or whether it is hind-before,
Remains obscure for evermore.
Philosophy, with head of snow,
Confesses that it does not know;
Logicians have debated long,
Which is the right end, which the wrong;
But all their efforts are in vain.
They will not ever ascertain.

A. E. HOUSMAN

WOBBLE-DEE-WOO

What would you do
With a Wobble-de-woo?
Would you eat it
Or wear it
Or play it?
What would you do
With a Wobble-dee-woo?
(I've only just learned
How to say it.)

What would you do
With a Wobble-dee-woo?
Would you wear it
Or play it
Or eat it?
What would you do
With a Wobble-dee-woo?
(I'm sorry, I'll have
To repeat it.)

What would you do
With a Wobble-dee-woo?
Would you play it
Or eat it
Or wear it?
What would you do
With a Wobble-dee-woo?
(It's driving me mad,
I can't bear it!)

COLIN WEST

FROM NUMBER NINE, PENWIPER MEWS

From Number Nine, Penwiper Mews,
There is really abominable news:
    They've discovered a head
    In the box for the bread,
But nobody seems to know whose.

EDWARD GOREY

THE AHKOND OF SWAT

Who, or why, or which, or *what*,
                    Is the Ahkond of Swat?

Is he tall or short, or dark or fair?
Does he sit on a stool or sofa or chair, or Squat,
                    The Ahkond of Swat?

Is he wise or foolish, young or old?
Does he drink his soup and his coffee cold, or Hot,
                    The Ahkond of Swat?

Does he sing or whistle, jabber or talk,
And when riding abroad does he gallop or walk,
                              or Trot,
                    The Ahkond of Swat?

Does he wear a turban, a fez or a hat?
Does he sleep on a mattress, a bed or a mat,
                              or a Cot,
                    The Ahkond of Swat?

When he writes a copy in round-hand size,
Does he cross his t's and finish his i's with a Dot,
                         The Ahkond of Swat?

Can he write a letter concisely clear,
Without a speck or a smudge or smear or Blot,
                         The Ahkond of Swat?

Do his people like him extremely well?
Or do they, whenever they can, rebel, or Plot,
                    At the Ahkond of Swat?

If he catches them then, either old or young,
Does he have them chopped in pieces or hung,
                                    or Shot,
                    The Ahkond of Swat?

Do his people prig in the lanes or park?
Or even at times, when days are dark, Garotte?
                         Oh, the Ahkond of Swat?

Does he study the wants of his own dominion?
Or doesn't he care for public opinion a Jot,
                         The Ahkond of Swat?

To amuse his mind do his people show him
Pictures, or any one's last new poem, or What,
                      For the Ahkond of Swat?

At night if he suddenly screams and wakes,
Do they bring him only a few small cakes, or a Lot,
                      For the Ahkond of Swat?

Does he live on turnips, tea or tripe,
Does he like his shawl to be marked with a stripe
                            or a Dot,
                    The Ahkond of Swat?

Does he like to lie on his back in a boat
Like the lady who lived in that isle remote, Shalott.
                    The Ahkond of Swat?

Is he quiet, or always making a fuss?
Is his steward a Swiss or a Swede or a Russ,
                                        or a Scot,
                        The Ahkond of Swat?

Does he like to sit by the calm blue wave?
Or to sleep and snore in a dark green cave,
                                        or a Grott,
                        The Ahkond of Swat?

Does he drink small beer from a silver jug?
Or a bowl? or a glass? or a cup? or a mug? or a Pot,
                        The Ahkond of Swat?

Does he beat his wife with a gold-topped pipe,
When she lets the gooseberries grow too ripe, or Rot,
                        The Ahkond of Swat?

Does he wear a white tie when he dines with his
    friends,
And tie it neat in a bow with ends, or a Knot,
                        The Ahkond of Swat?

Does he like new cream, and hate mince-pies?
When he looks at the sun does he wink his eyes,
                              or Not,
                    The Ahkond of Swat?

Does he teach his subjects to roast and bake?
Does he sail about on an inland lake, in a Yacht,
                    The Ahkond of Swat?

Some one, or nobody knows I wot
Who or which or why or what
          Is the Ahkond of Swat!

EDWARD LEAR

AS I WENT OVER THE WATER

As I went over the water,
   The water went over me.
I saw two little blackbirds
   Sitting on a tree:
The one called me a rascal,
   The other called me a thief;
I took up my little black stick,
   And knocked out all their teeth.

ANONYMOUS

THERE WAS AN OLD MAN WITH A BEARD

There was an Old Man with a beard,
Who said, 'It is just as I feared! –
Two Owls and a Hen, four Larks and a Wren,
Have all built their nests in my beard!'

EDWARD LEAR

THERE WAS AN OLD MAN OF DUMBREE

There was an Old Man of Dumbree,
who taught little Owls to drink Tea;
For he said,
'To eat mice is not proper or nice,'
That amiable Man of Dumbree.

EDWARD LEAR

POOEM

I, too, once hoped to have a hoopoe
Wing its way within my scoopoe,
Crested, quick, and heliotroopoe,
Proud *Upupa epops*.
For what seemed an eternity,
I sat upon a grassy sloopoe,
Gazing through a telescoopoe,
Weaving snares of finest roopoe,
Fit for *Upupa epops*.
At last, one day, there came to me,
Inside a crusty enveloopoe,
This note: 'Abandon hope, you doopoe;
The hoopoe is a misanthroopoe.
(Sighed) Your far-off friend, *U. e.*'

JOHN UPDIKE

THE DUCK

I hope you may have better luck
Than to be bitten by the Duck.

This bird is generally tame,
But he is dangerous all the same;

And though he looks so small and weak,
He has a very powerful beak.

Between the hours of twelve and two
You never know what he may do.

And sometimes he plays awkward tricks
From half-past four to half-past six.

And any hour of the day
It's best to keep out of his way.

LORD ALFRED DOUGLAS

GOOSEY, GOOSEY, GANDER

Goosey, goosey, gander,
  Where shall I wander?
Upstairs, downstairs,
  And in my lady's chamber.
There I met an old man
  Who would not say his prayers;
I took him by the left leg
  And threw him down the stairs.

ANONYMOUS

LITTLE BIRDS

Little Birds are dining
 Warily and well
 Hid in mossy cell:
Hid, I say, by waiters
Gorgeous in their gaiters –
 I've a Tale to tell.

Little Birds are feeding
 Justices with jam,
 Rich in frizzled ham:
Rich, I say, in oysters –
Haunting shady cloisters –
 That is what I am.

Little Birds are teaching
 Tigresses to smile,
 Innocent of guile:
Smile, I say, not smirkle –
Mouth a semicircle,
 That's the proper style!

Little Birds are sleeping
    All among the pins,
    Where the loser wins:
Where, I say, he sneezes,
When and how he pleases –
    So the Tale begins.

Little Birds are writing
    Interesting books,
    To be read by cooks;
Read, I say, not roasted –
Letterpress, when toasted,
    Loses its good looks.

Little Birds are seeking
    Hecatombs of haws,
    Dressed in snowy gauze:
Dressed, I say, in fringes
Half-alive with hinges –
    Thus they break the laws.

Little Birds are playing
    Bagpipes on the shore,
    Where the tourists snore:
'Thanks!' they cry. ''Tis thrilling.
Take, oh, take this shilling!
    Let us have no more!'

Little Birds are bathing
    Crocodiles in cream,
    Like a happy dream:
Like, but not so lasting –
Crocodiles, when fasting,
    Are not all they seem!

Little Birds are choking
    Baronets with bun,
    Taught to fire a gun:

Taught, I say, to splinter
Salmon in the winter –
    Merely for the fun.

Little Birds are hiding
    Crimes in carpet-bags,
    Blessed by happy stags:
Blessed, I say, though beaten –
Since our friends are eaten
    When the memory flags.

Little Birds are tasting
    Gratitude and gold,
    Pale with sudden cold;
Pale, I say, and wrinkled –
When the bells have tinkled,
    And the Tale is told.

LEWIS CARROLL

EVER SEE

Ever see
a flamingo
dance?

Passion
and romance
is what they adore

In the flash
of an eye
they take to the floor

Castanets
they click
with a flick of their bills

Then
paso doble
till pink in the gills

Flamingoes rule. Olé!

ROGER MCGOUGH

174

SPEAK ROUGHLY TO YOUR LITTLE BOY

THE DUCHESS'S LULLABY

Speak roughly to your little boy,
  And beat him when he sneezes:
He only does it to annoy,
  Because he knows it teases.

CHORUS
Wow! wow! wow!

I speak severely to my boy,
  I beat him when he sneezes;
For he can thoroughly enjoy
  The pepper when he pleases!

CHORUS
Wow! wow! wow!

LEWIS CARROLL

FRANKLIN HYDE,

Who caroused in the Dirt and was corrected by His Uncle.

His Uncle came on Franklin Hyde
Carousing in the Dirt.

He Shook him hard from Side to Side
And
Hit him till it Hurt,

Exclaiming, with a Final Thud,
'Take that! Abandoned Boy!
For Playing with Disgusting Mud
As though it were a Toy!'

MORAL
From Franklin Hyde's adventure, learn
To pass your Leisure Time
In Cleanly Merriment, and turn
From Mud and Ooze and Slime
And every form of Nastiness –
But, on the other Hand,
Children in ordinary Dress
May always play with Sand.

HILAIRE BELLOC

THE HAPPY FAMILY

Before the children say goodnight,
    Mother, Father, stop and think:
Have you screwed their heads on tight?
    Have you washed their ears with ink?

Have you said and done and thought
    All that earnest parents should?
Have you beat them as you ought:
    Have you begged them to be good?

And above all – when you start
    Out the door and douse the light –
Think, be certain, search your heart:
    Have you screwed their heads on tight?

If they sneeze when they're asleep,
    Will their little heads come off?
If they just breathe very deep?
    If – especially – they cough?

Should – alas! – the little dears
   Lose a little head or two,
Have you inked their little ears:
   Girls' ears pink and boys' ears blue?

Children's heads are very loose.
   Mother, Father, screw them tight.
If you feel uncertain use
   A monkey wrench, but do it right.

If a head should come unscrewed
    You will know that you have failed.
Doubtful cases should be glued.
    Stubborn cases should be nailed.

Then when all your darlings go
    Sweetly screaming off to bed,
Mother, Father, you may know
    Angels guard each little head.

Come the morning you will find
    One by one each little head
Full of gentle thought and kind,
    Sweetly screaming to be fed.

JOHN CIARDI

POLITENESS

My cousin John was most polite;
  He led shortsighted Mrs Bond,
By accident, one winter's night
  Into a village pond.
Her life perhaps he might have saved
But how genteelly he behaved!

Each time she rose and waved to him
  He smiled and bowed and doffed his hat;
Thought he, although I cannot swim,
  At least I can do that –
And when for the third time she sank
He stood bareheaded on the bank.

Be civil, then, to young and old;
  Especially to persons who
Possess a quantity of gold
  Which they might leave to you.
The more they have, it seems to me,
The more polite you ought to be.

HARRY GRAHAM

THE WILLOW-TREE

Long by the willow-tree
   Vainly they sought her,
Wild rang the mother's screams
   O'er the gray water.
'Where is my lovely one?
   Where is my daughter?

'Rouse thee, sir constable –
   Rouse thee and look.
Fisherman, bring your net,
   Boatman, your hook;
Beat in the lily beds,
   Dive in the brook.'

Vainly the constable
   Shouted and called her;
Vainly the fisherman
   Beat the green alder;
Vainly he threw the net,
   Never it hauled her!

Mother beside the fire
    Sat, her night-cap in;
Father, in easy chair,
    Gloomily napping;
When at the window-sill
    Came a light tapping.

And a pale countenance
    Looked through the casement:
Loud beat the mother's heart,
    Sick with amazement,
And at the vision which
    Came to surprise her!
Shrieking in an agony –
    'Lor! it's Elizar!'

Yes, 'twas Elizabeth;
    Yes, 'twas their girl;
Pale was her cheek, and her
    Hair out of curl.
'Mother!' the loved one,
    Blushing, exclaimed,
'Let not your innocent
    Lizzy be blamed.

'Yesterday, going to Aunt
    Jones's to tea,
Mother, dear mother, I
    Forgot the door-key!
And as the night was cold,
    And the way steep,
Mrs Jones kept me to
    Breakfast and sleep.'

Whether her pa and ma
    Fully believed her,
That we shall never know;
    Stern they received her;
And for the work of that
    Cruel, though short night, –
Sent her to bed without
    Tea for a fortnight.

Moral

Hey diddle diddlety,
   Cat and the fiddlety,
Maidens of England take
   Caution by she!
   Let love and suicide
   Never tempt you aside,
And always remember to take the door-key.

WILLIAM MAKEPEACE THACKERAY

PURPLE WILLIAM OR, THE LIAR'S DOOM

The hideous hue which William is
Was not originally his:
So long as William told the truth
He was a usual-coloured youth.

He now is purple. One fine day
His tender father chanced to say
'What colour is a whelp, and why?'
'Purple' was William's false reply.

'Pooh' said his Pa, 'You silly elf,
'It's no more purple than yourself.
'Dismiss the notion from your head.'
'I, too, am purple' William said.

And he *was* purple. With a yell
His mother off the sofa fell
Exclaiming 'William's purple! Oh!'
William replied 'I told you so.'

His parents, who could not support
The pungency of this retort,
Died with a simultaneous groan.
The purple orphan was alone.

A. E. HOUSMAN

INCONSIDERATE HANNAH

Naughty little Hannah said
She could make her Grandma whistle,
So, that night, inside her bed,
Placed some nettles and a thistle.

Though dear Grandma quite infirm is,
Heartless Hannah watched her settle,
With her poor old epidermis
Resting up against a nettle.

Suddenly she reached the thistle!
My! you should have heard her whistle!

A successful plan was Hannah's
But I cannot praise her manners.

HARRY GRAHAM

DEPARTMENT OF FACTS AND QUERIES

An Unexpected Fact

If down his throat a man should choose
    In fun, to jump or slide,
He'd scrape his shoes against his teeth,
    Nor soil his own inside.
But if his teeth were lost and gone,
And not a stump to scrape upon,
He'd see at once how very pat
His tongue lay there, by way of mat,
And he would wipe his feet on *that*!

EDWARD CANNON

SCIENTIFIC PROOF

If we square a lump of pemmican
　And cube a pot of tea,
Divide a musk ox by the span
　From noon to half-past three;
If we calculate the Eskimo
　By solar parallax,
Divide the sextant by a floe
　And multiply the cracks
By nth-powered igloos, we may prove
　All correlated facts.

If we prolongate the parallel
　Indefinitely forth,
And cube a sledge till we can tell
　The real square root of North;
Bisect a seal and bifurcate
　The tangent with a pack
Of Polar ice, we get the rate
　Along the Polar track,
And proof of corollary things
　Which otherwise we lack.

If we multiply the Arctic night
  By X times ox times moose,
And build an igloo on the site
  Of its hypotenuse;
If we circumscribe an arc about
  An Arctic dog and weigh
A segment of it, every doubt
  Is made as clear as day,
We also get the price of ice
  F.O.B. Baffin's Bay.

If we amplify the Arctic breeze
  By logarithmic signs,
And run through the isosceles
  Imaginary lines,
We find that twice the half of one
  Is equal to the whole.
Which, when the calculus is done,
  Quite demonstrates the Pole.
It also gives its length and breadth
  And what's the price of coal.

J. W. FOLEY

THE FLIES CRAWLED UP THE WINDOW

The flies crawled up the window
It's all they have to do
They went up by their thousands
and came down two by two

The flies crawled up the window
They said we love to roam
So once more up the window
and then we'll all go home

The flies crawled up the window
in sunshine and in rain
They do not seek for pleasure
They much prefer the pain

The flies crawled up the window
And yet the fact remains
You'll often meet with people
Who say flies have no brains

Next time you see flies crawling
Upside down upon a shelf
If you don't think that's clever
Just try it for yourself

ELLIS AND FURBER

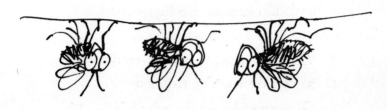

THE LAZY ROOF

The Roof it has a Lazy Time
   A-lying in the Sun;
  The Walls they have to Hold Him Up;
They do Not Have Much Fun!

GELETT BURGESS

STRANGE MEETING

Dear Madam,
> I'm sure you'll be happy to know
I'll be at the station at three.
But since we last met such a long time ago
You may well not guess which is me.

And so, to ensure that I'm easy to spot,
I'll dress in a pale lilac suit
And carry an elegant plant in a pot
(Or, if not, a basket of fruit).

Your eye will be caught by my red satin cape
Which flashes like flame in the light;
My cane will be wreathed in a length of black crepe.
I think you should know me all right.

And yet, just in case this is not quite enough
To give you the help that you need,
I'll put on my sword and my white pleated ruff,
And hold a small pig on a lead.

My Chinese attendants should give you a clue,
If still there's a doubt when we meet:
The face of the taller is painted bright blue;
The smaller has gloves on his feet.

The smoke from my ears isn't easy to miss;
My aftershave's Essence of Goat.
And, as for yourself, can you please tell me this:
Do you still glue balloons to your coat?

JOHN YEOMAN

CAPACITY

CAPACITY 26 PASSENGERS

– sign in a bus

Affable, bibulous,
corpulent, dull,
eager-to-find-a-seat,
formidable,
garrulous, humorous,
icy, jejune,
knockabout, laden-
with-luggage (maroon),
mild-mannered, narrow-necked,
oval-eyed, pert,
querulous, rakish,
seductive, tart, vert-
iginous, willowy,
xanthic (or yellow),
young, zebuesque are my
passengers fellow.

JOHN UPDIKE

FATHER WILLIAM

'You are old, Father William,' the young man said,
    'And your hair has become very white;
And yet you incessantly stand on your head –
    Do you think, at your age, it is right?'

'In my youth,' Father William replied to his son,
    'I feared it might injure the brain;
But, now that I'm perfectly sure I have none,
    Why, I do it again and again.'

'You are old,' said the youth, 'as I mentioned before,
    And have grown most uncommonly fat;
Yet you turned a back-somersault in at the door –
    Pray, what is the reason of that?'

'In my youth,' said the sage, as he shook his grey
    locks,
        'I kept all my limbs very supple
By the use of this ointment – one shilling the box –
    Allow me to sell you a couple?'

'You are old,' said the youth, 'and your jaws are too
    weak
        For anything tougher than suet;
Yet you finished the goose, with the bones and the
    beak –
        Pray, how did you manage to do it?'

'In my youth,' said his father, 'I took to the law,
    And argued each case with my wife;
And the muscular strength, which it gave to my jaw,
    Has lasted the rest of my life.'

'You are old,' said the youth, 'one would hardly
  suppose
    That your eye was as steady as ever;
Yet you balanced an eel on the end of your nose –
    What made you so awfully clever?'

'I have answered three questions, and that is
  enough,'
    Said his father; 'don't give yourself airs!
Do you think I can listen all day to such stuff?
    Be off, or I'll kick you down stairs!'

LEWIS CARROLL

THE SEA SERPANT
An Accurate Description

A-sleepin' at length on the sand,
  Where the beach was all tidy and clean,
A-strokin' his scale with the brush on his tail
  The wily Sea Serpant I seen.

And what was his colour? you asks,
  And how did he look? inquires you,
I'll be busted and blessed if he didn't look jest
  Like you would of expected 'im to!

His head was the size of a – well,
  The size what they always attains;
He whistled a tune what was built like a prune,
  And his tail was the shape o' his brains.

His scales they was ruther – you know –
  Like the leaves what you pick off o' eggs;
And the way o' his walk – well, it's useless to talk,
  Fer o' course you've seen Sea Serpants' legs.

His length it was seventeen miles,
   Or fathoms, or inches, or feet
(Me memory's sich that I can't recall which,
   Though at figgers I've seldome been beat).

And I says as I looks at the beast,
   'He reminds me o' somethin' I've seen –
Is it candy or cats or humans or hats,
   Or Fenimore Cooper I mean?'

And as I debated the point,
   In a way that I can't understand,
The Sea Serpant he disappeared in the sea
   And walked through the ocean by land.

And somehow I knowed he'd come back,
    So I marked off the place with me cap;
'Twas Latitude West and Longitude North
    And forty-eight cents by the map.

And his length it was seventeen miles,
    Or inches, or fathoms, or feet
(Me memory's sich that I can't recall which,
    Though at figgers I've seldom been beat).

WALLACE IRWIN

There was an old man in a trunk,
Who inquired of his wife, 'Am I drunk?'
She replied with regret,
'I'm afraid so, my pet.'
And he answered, 'It's just as I thunk.'

OGDEN NASH

THE WHITE KNIGHT'S BALLAD

I'll tell thee everything I can;
　　There's little to relate.
I saw an aged aged man,
　　A-sitting on a gate.
'Who are you, aged man?' I said.
　　'And how is it you live?'
And his answer trickled through my head
　　Like water through a sieve.

He said 'I look for butterflies
　　That sleep among the wheat:
I make them into mutton-pies,
　　And sell them in the street.
I sell them unto men,' he said,
　　'Who sail on stormy seas;
And that's the way I get my bread –
　　A trifle, if you please.'

But I was thinking of a plan
 To dye one's whiskers green,
And always use so large a fan
 That they could not be seen.
So, having no reply to give
 To what the old man said,
I cried 'Come, tell me how you live!'
 And thumped him on the head.

His accents mild took up the tale:
 He said 'I go my ways,
And when I find a mountain-rill,
 I set it in a blaze;
And thence they make a stuff they call
 Rowland's Macassar Oil –
Yet twopence-halfpenny is all
 They give me for my toil.'

But I was thinking of a way
    To feed oneself on batter,
And so go on from day to day
    Getting a little fatter.
I shook him well from side to side,
    Until his face was blue:
'Come, tell me how you live,' I cried
    'And what it is you do!'

He said 'I hunt for haddocks' eyes
    Among the heather bright,
And work them into waistcoat-buttons
    In the silent night.
And these I do not sell for gold
    Or coin of silvery shine,
But for a copper halfpenny,
    And that will purchase nine.

'I sometimes dig for buttered rolls,
    Or set limed twigs for crabs;
I sometimes search the grassy knolls
    For wheels of hansom-cabs.

And that's the way' (he gave a wink)
  'By which I get my wealth –
And very gladly will I drink
  Your Honour's noble health.'

I heard him then, for I had just
  Completed my design
To keep the Menai bridge from rust
  By boiling it in wine.
I thanked him much for telling me
  The way he got his wealth.
But chiefly for his wish that he
  Might drink my noble health.

And now, if e'er by chance I put
  My fingers into glue,
Or madly squeeze a right-hand foot
  Into a left-hand shoe
Or if I drop upon my toe
  A very heavy weight,
I weep, for it reminds me so
Of that old man I used to know –
Whose look was mild, whose speech was
  slow,

Whose hair was whiter than the snow,
Whose face was very like a crow,
With eyes, like cinders, all aglow,
Who seemed distracted with his woe,
Who rocked his body to and fro,
And muttered mumblingly and low,
As if his mouth were full of dough,
Who snorted like a buffalo –
That summer evening long ago
   A-sitting on a gate.

LEWIS CARROLL

PLANTING A MAILBOX

Prepare the ground when maple buds have burst
And when the daytime moon is sliced so thin
His fibers drink blue sky with litmus thirst.
This moment come, begin.

The site should be within an easy walk,
Beside a road, in stony earth. Your strength
Dictates how deep you delve. The seedling's stalk
Should show three feet of length.

Don't harrow, weed, or water; just apply
A little gravel. Sun, and motor fumes
Perform the miracle; in late July,
A young post office blooms.

JOHN UPDIKE

TRIOLET

I wish I were a jelly fish
That cannot fall downstairs:
Of all the things I wish to wish
I wish I were a jelly fish
That hasn't any cares,
And doesn't even have to wish
'I wish I were a jelly fish
That cannot fall downstairs.'

G. K. CHESTERTON

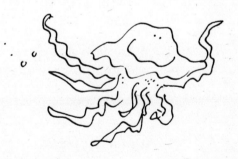

POEMS OF MYSTERY AND IMAGINATION
(No. 1)

Goldfish
are not
boldfish

They cry
when they
fall over

They tittletat
and chew
the fat

And are glad
when it's
all over.

ROGER MCGOUGH

THE SWORD-FISH

The Sword-fish is an awful brute,
He tears your hair out by the root.

And when you're bathing in the sea,
He leaps upon you suddenly.

And if you get out on the sand,
He sometimes follows you inland.

LORD ALFRED DOUGLAS

THE COD

There's something very strange and odd
About the habits of the Cod.

For when you're swimming in the sea,
He sometimes bites you on the knee.

And though his bites are not past healing,
It is a most unpleasant feeling.

And when you're diving down below,
He often nips you on the toe.

And though he doesn't hurt you much,
He has a disagreeable touch.

There's one thing to be said for him, –
It is a treat to see him swim.

But though he swims in graceful curves,
He rather gets upon your nerves.

LORD ALFRED DOUGLAS

AFTERNOON OF A PRAWN

I don't mind dawn.
Night comes and goes.
It's afternoon
Gets up my nose.

I wish I'd not
Been born a prawn.
I'd sooner be
A unicorn

Complete with horn,
But no such luck.
Wouldn't have minded
Being a duck –

At least I'd quack –
But all around
The salty seas
Prawns make no sound,

But a thin whistle,
A tedious song,
And afternoons
Grow far too long.

Nothing to do
With your see-through shell.
Afternoons
For prawns are hell.

I don't mind dawn.
Night comes and goes.
It's afternoons
Get up my nose.

KIT WRIGHT

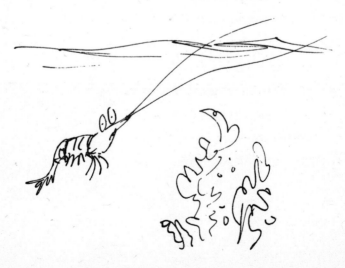

IT MAKES A CHANGE

There's nothing makes a Greenland whale
Feel half so high and mighty
As sitting on a mantelpiece
In Aunty Mabel's nighty.

It makes a change from Freezing Seas,
(Of which a whale can tire),
To warm his weary tail at ease
Before an English fire.

For this delight he leaves the seas
(Unknown to Aunty Mabel),
Returning only when the dawn
Lights up the Breakfast Table.

MERVYN PEAKE

STICKY ENDS

THE BABE

The babe, with a cry brief and dismal,
Fell into the water baptismal:
E're they'd gathered its plight,
It had sunk out of sight,
For the depth of the font was abysmal.

EDWARD GOREY

LITTLE WILLIE'S DEAD

Little Willie's dead,
Jam him in the coffin,
For you don't get the chance
Of a funeral of'en.

ANONYMOUS

227

THE LION

Oh, weep for Mr and Mrs Bryan!
He was eaten by a lion;
Following which, the lion's lioness
Up and swallowed Bryan's Bryaness.

OGDEN NASH

WASTE

I had written to Aunt Maud,
Who was on a trip abroad,
　　When I heard she'd died of cramp
　　Just too late to save the stamp.

HARRY GRAHAM

IDYLL

I knew a child called Alma Brent,
   Completely destitute of brains,
Whose principal accomplishment
Was imitating railway trains.

When ladies called at 'Sunnyside',
Mama, to keep the party clean,
Would say, with pardonable pride,
   'Now, Alma, do the six-fifteen.'

The child would grunt and snort and puff,
   With weird contortions of the face,
And when the guests had had enough,
   She'd cease, with one last wild grimace.

One day her jovial Uncle Paul
   Cried, 'Come on, Alma! Do your worst!'
And, challenged thus before them all,
   She did the four-nineteen – and burst.

J. B. MORTON

SALLY SIMPKIN'S LAMENT OR, JOHN JONES'S KIT-CAT-ASTROPHE

'Oh! what is that comes gliding in,
   And quite in middling haste?
It is the picture of my Jones,
   And painted to the waist.

'It is not painted to the life,
   For where's the trowsers blue?
Oh Jones, my dear! – Oh dear! my Jones,
   What is become of you?'

'Oh! Sally dear, it is too true, –
    The half that you remark
Is come to say my other half
    Is bit off by a shark!

'Oh! Sally, sharks do things by halves,
    Yet most completely do!
A bite in one place seems enough,
    But I've been bit in two.

'You know I once was all your own,
    But now a shark must share!
But let that pass – for now to you
    I'm neither here nor there.

'Alas! death has a strange divorce
    Effected in the sea,
It has divided me from you,
    And even me from me!

'Don't fear my ghost will walk 'o nights
    To haunt as people say;
My ghost *can't* walk, for, oh! my legs
    Are many leagues away!

'Lord! think when I am swimming round,
    And looking where the boat is,
A shark just snaps away a *half*,
    Without 'a *quarter*'s notice'.

'One half is here, the other half
    Is near Columbia placed;
Oh! Sally, I have got the whole
    Atlantic for my waist.

'But now, adieu – a long adieu!
    I've solved death's awful riddle,
And would say more, but I am doomed
    To break off in the middle.'

THOMAS HOOD

ON THE ACCIDENTAL DEATH OF AN OFFICER OF THE SALVATION ARMY

'Hallelujah!' was the only observation
That escaped Lieutenant-Colonel Mary Jane,
When she tumbled off the platform in the station,
And was cut in little pieces by the train.
    Mary Jane, the train is through yer:
    Hallelujah, Hallelujah!
We will gather up the fragments that remain.

A. E. HOUSMAN

KITTY

Isn't it a
Dreadful pity
What became of
Dreamy Kitty,
Noticing the
Moon above her,
Not
  the
    missing
      man-hole
       cover?

COLIN WEST

DISTRACTING CREATURES

Said the monkey to the donkey,
'What'll you have to drink?'
Said the donkey to the monkey,
'I'd like a swig of ink.'

ANONYMOUS

A Cat Came Dancing out of a Barn

A cat came dancing out of a barn
With a pair of bag-pipes under her arm;
She could sing nothing but, Fiddle cum fee,
The mouse has married the bumble-bee.
Pipe, cat; dance, mouse;
We'll have a wedding at our good house.

Nursery Rhyme

THE COMIC ADVENTURES OF OLD MOTHER HUBBARD AND HER DOG

Old Mother Hubbard
Went to the cupboard,
To fetch her poor dog a bone;
But when she came there
The cupboard was bare
And so the poor dog had none.

She went to the baker's
To buy him some bread;
But when she came back
The poor dog was dead.

She went to the undertaker's
To buy him a coffin;
But when she came back
The poor dog was laughing.

She took a clean dish
  To get him some tripe:
But when she came back
  He was smoking a pipe.

She went to the alehouse
  To get him some beer;
But when she came back
  The dog sat in a chair.

She went to the tavern
  For white wine and red;
But when she came back
  The dog stood on his head.

She went to the fruiterer's
  To buy him some fruit;
But when she came back
  He was playing the flute.

She went to the tailor's
    To buy him a coat;
But when she came back
He was riding a goat.

She went to the hatter's
    To buy him a hat;
But when she came back
    He was feeding the cat.

She went to the barber's
    To buy him a wig;
But when she came back
    He was dancing a jig.

She went to the cobbler's
   To buy him some shoes:
But when she came back
   He was reading the news.

She went to the seamstress
   To buy him some linen;
But when she came back
   The dog was a-spinning.

She went to the hosier's
   To buy him some hose;
But when she came back
   He was dressed in his clothes.

The dame made a curtsey,
   The dog made a bow;
The dame said, Your servant,
   The dog said, Bow-wow.

ANONYMOUS

NINE MICE

Nine mice on tiny tricycles
went riding on the ice,
they rode in spite of warning signs,
they rode despite advice.

The signs were right, the ice was thin,
in half a trice, the mice fell in,
and from their chins down to their toes,
those mice entirely froze.

Nine mindless mice, who paid the price,
are thawing slowly by the ice,
still sitting on their tricycles
. . . nine white and shiny *micicles!*

JACK PRELUTSKY

VLADIMIR'S SONG *from* '*WAITING FOR GODOT*'

A dog came into the kitchen
And stole a crust of bread.
Then cook up with a ladle
And beat him till he was dead.

Then all the dogs came running
And dug the dog a tomb
And wrote upon the tombstone
For the eyes of dogs to come:

A dog came in the kitchen
And stole a crust of bread.
Then cook up with a ladle
And beat him till he was dead.

Then all the dogs came running
And dug the dog a tomb
And wrote upon the tombstone
For the eyes of dogs to come:

SAMUEL BECKETT

OLD MOTHER HUBBARD AND HER DOG REVISITED

Said Old Mother Hubbard, one dark winter's night,
While giving a bath to her goat,
'That dog looks as though he's been having a fight:
I wish he'd take pride in his coat.'

The very next morning she had a great shock
Which made her feel weak at the knees,
For there was the dog, wearing beret and smock,
Painting pictures of birds in the trees.

He went indoors, leaving his paintings to dry;
She followed – and what do you think?
He was dressed as a sailor, a patch on one eye,
With a small fleet of boats in the sink.

Said Old Mother Hubbard, 'You're getting me
   down;
Oh, won't you behave yourself, please?'
But five minutes later, got up like a clown,
He was juggling with pieces of cheese.

So Old Mother Hubbard lay down to relax:
She felt a slight ache in the head.
But dressed as a burglar, with crowbar and axe,
The dog stole the legs off the bed.

Then Old Mother Hubbard heard no noise at all.
Now, did that mean mischief or not?
She found him downstairs, dressed in bonnet and
 shawl,
And gurgling away in his cot.

'Oh, do something useful!' the poor woman cried.
The dog scratched his head, thinking hard.
Then, in helmet and armour, he clattered outside,
Giving chase to the mice in the yard.

Thought Old Mother Hubbard, while bolting the
 door,
'He's so disobedient and rude!
But I won't pass remarks on his coat any more:
He's better behaved in the nude.'

JOHN YEOMAN

THE STORY OF THE MAN THAT WENT OUT SHOOTING

This is the man that shoots the hares;
This is the coat he always wears:
With game-bag, powder-horn and gun
He's going out to have some fun.

The hare sits snug in leaves and grass,
And laughs to see the green man pass.
He finds it hard, without a pair
Of spectacles, to shoot the hare.

Now, as the sun grew very hot,
And he a heavy gun had got,
He lay down underneath a tree
And went to sleep, as you may see.

And, while he slept like any top,
The little hare came, hop, hop, hop,
Took gun and spectacles, and then
On her hind legs went off again.

The green man wakes and sees her place
The spectacles upon her face;
And now she's trying all she can
To shoot the sleepy, green-coat man.

He cries and screams and runs away;
The hare runs after him all day,
And hears him call out everywhere:
'Help! Fire! Help! The Hare! The Hare!'

At last he stumbled at the well
Head over ears, and in he fell.
The hare stopp'd short, took aim, and hark!
Bang went the gun, – she miss'd her mark!
The poor man's wife was drinking up
Her coffee in her coffee-cup;
The gun shot cup and saucer through;
'O dear!' cried she, 'what shall I do?'

There liv'd close by the cottage there
The hare's own child, the little hare;
And while she stood upon her toes,
The coffee fell and burn'd her nose.
'O dear!' she cried, with spoon in hand,
'Such fun I do not understand.'

DR HEINRICH HOFFMAN

FUR AND FEATHERS

The Emus formed a football team
Up Walgett way;
Their dark-brown sweaters were a dream
But kangaroos would sit and scream
To watch them play.

'Now, butterfingers,' they would call,
And such-like names;
The emus couldn't hold the ball
– They had no hands – but hands aren't all
In football games.

A match against the kangaroos
They played one day.
The kangaroos were forced to choose
Some wallabies and wallaroos
That played in grey.

The rules that in the West prevail
Would shock the town;
For when a kangaroo set sail
An emu jumped upon his tail
And fetched him down.

A whistler duck as referee
Was not admired.
He whistled so incessantly
The teams rebelled, and up a tree
He soon retired.

The old marsupial captain said
'It's do or die!'
So down the ground like fire he fled
And leaped above an emu's head
And scored a try.

Then shouting 'Keep it on the toes!'
The emus came.
Fierce as the flooded Bogan flows
They laid their foemen out in rows
And saved the game.

On native pear and Darling pea
They dined that night:
But one man was an absentee:
The whistler duck – their referee –
Had taken flight.

A. B. 'BANJO' PATERSON

THE MONKEY'S GLUE

When the monkey in his madness
  Took the glue to mend his voice,
'Twas the crawfish showed his sadness
  That the bluebird could rejoice.

Then the perspicacious parrot
  Sought to save the suicide
By administering carrot,
  But the monkey merely died.

So the crawfish and the parrot
  Sauntered slowly toward the sea,
While the bluebird stole the carrot
  And returned the glue to me.

GOLDWIN GOLDSMITH

THE MONKEY'S WEDDING

The monkey married the Baboon's sister,
Smacked his lips and then he kissed her,
He kissed so hard he raised a blister.
　　　She set up a yell.
The bridesmaid stuck on some court plaster,
It stuck so fast it couldn't stick faster,
Surely 'twas a sad disaster,
　　　But it soon got well.

What do you think the bride was dressed in?
White gauze veil and a green glass breast-pin,
Red kid shoes – she was quite interesting,
　　　She was quite a belle.
The bridegroom swell'd with a blue shirt collar,
Black silk stock that cost a dollar,
Large false whiskers the fashion to follow;
　　　He cut a monstrous swell.

What do you think they had for supper?
Black-eyed peas and bread and butter,
Ducks in the duck-house all in a flutter,
      Pickled oysters too.
Chestnuts raw and boil'd and roasted,
Apples sliced and onions toasted,
Music in the corner posted,
      Waiting for the cue.

What do you think was the tune they danced to?
'The drunken Sailor' – sometimes 'Jim Crow,'
Tails in the way – and some got pinched, too,
      'Cause they were too long.
What do you think they had for a fiddle?
An old Banjo with a hole in the middle,
A Tambourine made out of a riddle,
      And that's the end of my song.

ANONYMOUS

SIMPLE SIMON

Simple Simon went a-fishing
For to catch a whale;
All the water he had got
Was in his mother's pail.

Simple Simon went a-skating
On a pond in June.
'Dear me,' he cried, 'this water's wet,
I fear I've come too soon!'

Simple Simon made a snowball,
And brought it home to roast;
He laid it down before the fire,
And soon the ball was lost.

Simple Simon bought a gun,
'To shoot a bird,' he said.
He held the gun the wrong way round,
And shot himself instead.

ANONYMOUS

SCIENCE FOR THE YOUNG

Thoughtful little Willie Frazer
Carved his name with father's razor;
Father, unaware of trouble,
Used the blade to shave his stubble.
Father cut himself severely,
Which pleased little Willie dearly –
'I have fixed my father's razor
So it cuts!' said Willie Frazer.

Mamie often wondered why
Acids trouble alkali –
Mamie, in a manner placid,
Fed the cat boracic acid,
Whereupon the cat grew frantic,
Executing many an antic,
'Ah!' cried Mamie, overjoyed,
'Pussy is an alkaloid!'

Arthur with a lighted taper
Touched the fire to grandpa's paper.
Grandpa leaped a foot or higher,
Dropped the sheet and shouted 'Fire!'
Arthur, wrapped in contemplation,
Viewed the scene of conflagration.
'This,' he said, 'confirms my notion –
Heat creates both light and motion.'

Wee, experimental Nina
Dropped her mother's Dresden china
From a seventh-story casement,
Smashing, crashing to the basement.
Nina, somewhat apprehensive,
Said: 'This china is expensive,
Yet it proves by demonstration
Newton's law of gravitation.'

WALLACE IRWIN

HOORAY FOR CAPTAIN SPAULDING

Chorus:
Hooray for Captain Spaulding,
The African explorer!
Groucho:
Did someone call me schnorrer?
Chorus:
Hooray, hooray, hooray!

Chorus:
Hooray for Captain Spaulding,
The African explorer!
Groucho:
Did someone call me schnorrer?
Chorus:
Hooray, hooray, hooray!

Chorus:
He went into the jungle
Where all the monkeys throw nuts,
Groucho:
If I stay here I'll go nuts,
Chorus:
Hooray, hooray, hooray!

Chorus:
One day he caught a lion,
A tiger: and a monkey,
Groucho:
I thought it was a donkey,
Chorus:
Hooray, hooray, hooray!

Groucho:
I put all my reliance
In courage and defiance,
And risked my life for science,
Hey, Hey!
I had a guide named Streeter,
He lent me his repeater,
I bought down a mosquiter,
Hey, Hey!

Chorus:
One day in Madagascar
He bagged a dozen weasels
Groucho:
And all of them had measles,
Chorus:
Hooray, hooray, hooray!

Chorus:
Hooray for Captain Spaulding,
Whose name and fame are spreading
Groucho:
But who knows where it's heading?
Chorus:
Hooray, hooray,
Hooray! Hooray, hooray, hooray!

BERT KALMAR AND HARRY RUBY

THE ADVENTURES OF ISABEL

Isabel met an enormous bear,
Isabel, Isabel, didn't care;
The bear was hungry, the bear was ravenous,
The bear's big mouth was cruel and cavernous.
The bear said, Isabel, glad to meet you,
How do, Isabel, now I'll eat you!
Isabel, Isabel, didn't worry,
Isabel didn't scream or scurry,
She washed her hands and she straightened her hair
  up,
Then Isabel quietly ate the bear up.

Once in a night as black as pitch
Isabel met a wicked witch.
The witch's face was cross and wrinkled,
The witch's gums with teeth were sprinkled.
Ho ho, Isabel! the old witch crowed,
I'll turn you into an ugly toad!
Isabel, Isabel, didn't worry,
Isabel didn't scream or scurry,

She showed no rage, she showed no rancor,
But she turned the witch into milk and drank her.

Isabel met a hideous giant,
Isabel continued self-reliant.
The giant was hairy, the giant was horrid,
He had one eye in the middle of his forehead.
Good morning, Isabel, the giant said,
I'll grind your bones to make my bread.
Isabel, Isabel, didn't worry,
Isabel didn't scream or scurry.

She nibbled the zwieback that she always fed off,
And when it was gone, she cut the giant's head off.

Isabel met a troublesome doctor,
He punched and he poked till he really shocked her.
The doctor's talk was of coughs and chills
And the doctor's satchel bulged with pills.
The doctor said unto Isabel,
Swallow this, it will make you well.
Isabel, Isabel, didn't worry,
Isabel didn't scream or scurry.
She took those pills from the pill concoctor,
And Isabel calmly cured the doctor.

Isabel once was asleep in bed
When a horrible dream crawled into her head.
It was worse than a dinosaur, worse than a shark,
Worse than an octopus oozing in the dark.
'Boo!' said the dream, with a dreadful grin,
'I'm going to scare you out of your skin!'
Isabel, Isabel, didn't worry,
Isabel didn't scream or scurry,
Isabel had a cleverer scheme;
She just woke up and fooled that dream.

Whenever you meet a bugaboo
Remember what Isabel used to do.
Don't scream when the bugaboo says 'Boo!'
Just look it in the eye and say, 'Boo to you!'
That's how to banish a bugaboo;
Isabel did it and so can you!
Boooooo to you.

OGDEN NASH

KNOTS

Our son may be backward and lacking in graces
And virtually covered in spots,
But since the first day he could do up his laces
He's dazzled us all with his knots.
Why, only just now, with a speed that confused us,
He showed us a Granny and Reef.
His light-hearted patter informed and amused us,
His deftness was well past belief.

Without the least effort he fashioned, one-handed,
A Pineapple, Rope-Yarn and Slip;
He whipped up a fine Matthew Walker (eight-
    stranded)
And never once fumbled his grip.
His quick repartee really had us in stitches.
We gasped at that flexible wrist;
We thrilled to the skill of his Sennits and Hitches,
His Sheepshank, his quaint Monkey's Fist.

And then, in a trice and, it seemed, with no trouble
He tied, to the awe of our friends,
Some beautiful Blackwalls, both single and double,
Topped off with some Fisherman's Bends.
To finish the act he produced, without thinking,
A classically tight Wall-and-Crown.
He took a brief bow and he's now gone out drinking.
So, please, could you hoist us all down?

JOHN YEOMAN

BONES

Said Mr Smith, 'I really cannot
   Tell you, Dr Jones –
The most peculiar pain I'm in –
   I think it's in my *bones*.'

Said Dr Jones, 'Oh, Mr Smith,
   That's nothing. Without doubt
We have a simple cure for that;
   It is to take them out.'

He laid forthwith poor Mr Smith
   Close-clamped upon the table,
And, cold as stone, took out his bones
   As fast as he was able.

And Smith said, 'Thank you, thank you, *thank* you,'
   And wished him a Good-day;
And with his parcel 'neath his arm
   He slowly moved away.

WALTER DE LA MARE

THE RELUCTANT HERO OR, BAREFOOT IN THE SNOW

When he put on his socks in the morning
He found they were much too tight.
His feet, without any warning,
Had lengthened over night.
He didn't have any others,
He couldn't pick or choose.
He borrowed a pair of his mother's
And went to put on his shoes.

When he put on his shoes in the morning
He found they were much too tight.
His feet, without any warning,
Had lengthened in the night.
His toes and heels were skinned – oh,
His feet had grown like roots.
His shoes went out of the window
And he went to put on his boots.

When he put on his boots in the morning
He found they were much too tight.

His feet, without any warning,
Had lengthened over night.
His little toe was just in,
He had to squash and squeeze.
He threw them into the dust bin
And he went to put on his skis.

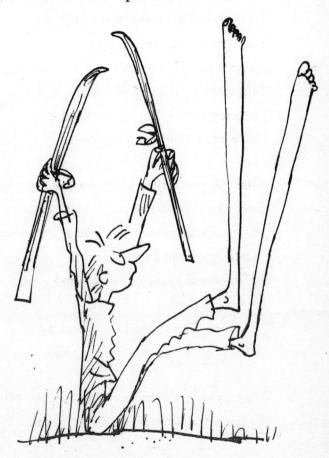

When he put on his skis in the morning
He found they were much too tight.
His feet, without any warning,
Had lengthened over night.
He had no footware which in
His feet could feel at ease.
The skis went into the kitchen
And his toes were left to freeze.

And so he went out barefoot,
No socks or shoes he wore.
He trod in places where foot
Had never trod before.
And everywhere his feet sent
A message to the sky.
His footprints down the street meant
A hero's passing by.

MARGARET MAHY

INDEX OF POETS

INDEX OF FIRST LINES

280

ACKNOWLEDGEMENTS

The editor and publishers gratefully acknowledge the following for permission to reproduce copyright poems in this book:

'Vladimir's Song' by Samuel Beckett from *Waiting for Godot*, published by Faber & Faber Ltd, and by Grove Press, Inc, US, 1954, copyright © Grove Press, Inc, 1954, renewed by Samuel Beckett, 1982, reprinted by permission of Faber & Faber Ltd, and Grove/Atlantic, Inc; 'The Road to Zoagli' by Max Beerbohm from *Men in Verse*, published by Stephen Greene Press, 1963, copyright © Mrs Eva Reichmann, reprinted by permission of Sir Rupert Hart-Davis on behalf of Eva Reichmann; 'The Yak' and 'Franklin Hyde' by Hilaire Belloc from *Complete Verse*, published by Pimlico, reprinted by permission of the Peters Fraser & Dunlop Group Ltd; 'The Island of Llince' from *Let's Marry Said the Cherry* by N. M. Bodecker, published by Faber & Faber Ltd, reprinted by permission of the publisher, and Tumbledown Editions; 'Mrs MacPhee' by Charles Causley from *Early in the Morning*, published by Viking Kestrel, 1986, copyright © Charles Causley, 1986, reprinted by permission of David Higham Associates; two extracts from *James and the Giant Peach* by Roald Dahl, published by Penguin Books Ltd, 1961, copyright © Felicity Dahl and the other Executors of the Estate of Roald Dahl, 1961, reprinted by permission of Murray Pollinger; 'The Cod', 'The Duck' and 'The Sword-fish' from *Lord Alfred Douglas' Animal Verse* by Lord Alfred Douglas, published by B. T. Batsford, copyright © Sheila Colman, Lord Alfred Douglas' Literary Estate, 1977, reprinted by permission of the publisher; 'The Flies Crawled up the Window' by Ellis and Furber from the film *Jack's the Boy* distributed by Rank Film Distributors Ltd, reprinted by courtesy of the Rank Organisation Plc; 'There's a Rather Odd Couple', 'From Number Nine Penwiper Mews', 'The Utter Zoo Alphabet' and 'The Babe' by Edward Gorey from *The Listing Attic*, published by Duell, Sloane & Pearce – Little, Brown, 1954, copyright © Edward Gorey, 1954, 1972, reprinted by permission of Donadio & Ashworth, Inc; 'Typo', 'Anfruca' and 'The Friendly Cinammon Bun' from *The Pedalling Man* by Russell Hoban, published by Heinemann, reprinted by permission of David Higham Associates; 'The Reluctant Hero', 'The Remarkable Cake' and 'Sensible Questions' from *Nonstop Nonsense* by Margaret Mahy, published by J. M. Dent & Sons Ltd, reprinted by permission of the publisher; 'Bones', 'Buttons' and 'Moonshine', by Walter de la Mare, reprinted by permission of The Literary Trustees of Walter de la Mare and The Society of Authors as their representative; 'Hooray for Captain Spaulding' by Bert Kalmar & Harry Ruby, published by Warner Chappell Music Ltd, London W1Y 3FA and Redwood Music Ltd, London NW1 8BD, copyright © 1956 Harms Inc, USA, reprinted by permission of International Music Publications Ltd; 'Gazebos' and 'Poems of Mystery and Imagination' by Roger McGough from *Nailing the Shadow*, published by Viking Kestrel, 1987,